party
cocktails

party
cocktails

Ian Wisniewski

special photography jan baldwin

conran
OCTOPUS

First published in 1999 by
Conran Octopus Limited
a part of Octopus Publishing Group
2–4 Heron Quays
London E14 4JP
www.conran-octopus.co.uk

This paperback edition published in 2002

Editorial consultant Jenni Muir
Managing editor Helen Ridge
Art editor Alison Barclay
Stylist Arabella McNie
Drinks for photography Meg Jansz
Picture research Clare Limpus
Production Oliver Jeffreys

A catalogue record for this book is
available from the British Library

ISBN 1 84091 290 1

Printed in China

*The recipes in this book are
intended solely for use by
responsible adults. Alcohol is
fine in moderation, but excess
consumption can damage your
health. Any recipes that call for
the flaming of alcohol should be
attempted only by sober adults,
and are undertaken at the maker's
own risk. Pregnant women, the
elderly, infants and those whose
immune systems are
compromised should avoid raw or
partially cooked eggs.*

contents

introduction

If only there were a completely reliable formula for success, then every party would be totally fabulous and we'd never have to endure another flop again. There are guidelines, of course, but following them doesn't provide any guarantees. Assembling a crowd of interesting guests is an advantage only if they actually mix, and serving great food is merely a consolation if your guests aren't having fun. Making sure everyone has enough to drink also entails an element of risk, as alcohol can inspire the worst as well as the best in people — including the hosts.

And there's one other vital consideration. If you're not in the mood, then no permutation of gorgeous guests, sensational canapés and cocktails, not to mention sequinned entertainment, will be enough. Oh, well. So, it doesn't always work out. So what? There are always more parties…

Sometimes the only drink on offer is a cup of tea, accompanied by a digestive biscuit, but it's still possible to have an instant party, as long as the mood is right and the conversation flows. Moreover, any location and set of circumstances can be elevated by the right drink. A Dry Martini or a Margarita can take me straight to that 'special zone', where any party can become the only place I want to be.

Despite the popular assumption that writing about drinks consists almost entirely of drinking, I spend far more time with a pen and notebook – or keyboard – in my hands than a glass. However, I do spend as much time as possible in cafés and bars wherever I travel. Seeing what's ordered, and how it's served, provides a short cut to an essential element of regional and national culture. This book explores some of the traditions and influences that have resulted in such a wide range of drinks, and also conveys some of the drinking rituals that have evolved around them. It is not intended to be a comprehensive reference book, but a guide to various drinks and the role they play in parties and celebrations around the world. Of course, I'll never be able to taste every type of drink, and certainly not in every combination, but I was able to draw on numerous trips and drinking sessions for the chapters that follow.

I generally prefer drinking spirits to wine and beer, with vodka being my first choice. As my family is Polish, I was brought up on a staple diet of vodka, in the sense that it was always around whenever we had guests. The Polish vodka industry is currently in overdrive, with around 1,000 brands on the market. No, I haven't tried them all, but I have visited the source of some of the finest. At the Zielona Gora distillery in western Poland, I saw how various clear and flavoured vodkas are produced. In Poznan I toured the largest rectification plant in Europe, but I couldn't understand why

this macho, all-male environment had calendars on the walls depicting fluffy cats, and bowls of milk. The calendars are an in-joke, the milk a genuine source of refreshment; so much grain is delivered for distillation at the plant that every mouse in the area heads over for a blow-out, which also explains why cats are a distiller's best friend.

Goulash, gypsy musicians and other tourist clichés that I hadn't previously experienced were my priorities on a recent visit to Budapest. My hosts gave me a wonderful insight into local life, including the leading brand of bitters, Zwack Unicum, which is distilled in the city. But I had to wait until the last night, when dinner and entertainment on a boat cruising the Danube delivered everything, particularly when a dancing troupe asked for volunteers.

I also tried Scottish dancing at a ceilidh that wrapped up a visit to some whisky distilleries. And there were plenty of disco classics, accompanied by bourbon and Coke, Manhattans and Mint Juleps at a gala dinner dance during the annual bourbon festival in Bardstown, Kentucky.

While visiting tequila distilleries in Mexico, I experienced working as a *jimador*, literally 'harvester'. The *jimadors*, in fact, undertake all aspects of cultivating agave plants, from which tequila is distilled. Planting, pruning, and harvesting agave by

slicing off the incredibly tough leaves, and hacking through the root system, can only be done manually and is very tough, skilled work. I gave it my best shot, but I know that I'll never be employed in that capacity.

At L'Altena, one of the most traditional tequila distilleries, I tasted freshly distilled tequila from a hollow bull's horn. This ritual dates from the time Spanish conquistadors drank from bulls' horns, in the absence of glasses. The large horn was full to the brim with distillation-strength tequila at 65 per cent abv, and it wasn't yet 11am. I took a small sip. 'Finish it,' urged my host. Down it went. And I went up, up and away. But at least I had taken part in a great tradition.

I love watching cocktails being prepared by a professional. The procession of ingredients, those precise, economical movements of shaking, stirring, pouring and garnishing – it's bar-counter choreography. And in my search for the truth, it's always illuminating to see a classic cocktail prepared in its original venue. Consequently, my enjoyment of a Bellini – champagne and peach purée – at Harry's Bar in Venice went beyond the academic.

There are three vital characteristics that a cocktail must have. It has to look good, even before it's brought to the table, ensuring that vital sense of anticipation; the aroma must be enticing; and, of course, the cocktail must deliver on the palate. While cocktails create an automatic sense of occasion, they're also about experimentation. You may decline a glass of kummel (caraway-flavoured spirit), for example, but you're more likely to accept a Silver Bullet – kummel with vodka.

The key to a successful cocktail party is, of course, a comprehensive shopping list to stock up on ingredients and accessories. Naturally, the finest ingredients yield the best results. Combining inferior ingredients may disguise them, but it can't elevate them. Similarly, recipes stating specific spirits are not a cue for approximation. Using bourbon or Irish whiskey in place of Scotch whisky will not give the same result.

A cocktail is also about balance. It may be very tempting to ignore the part of a recipe that calls for only a dash of some obscure ingredient, on the basis that such a small quantity won't make a difference. It will. If it seems extravagant to buy something that is merely used a dash at a time, then let it be an incentive to give cocktail parties more frequently.

Essential equipment includes an ice bucket, tongs and an abundant supply of ice, which can only be used once. A cocktail shaker and bar strainer, known as a hawthorn, as well as a stirring/mixing glass, or jug, and long stirring spoon enable you to shake just as readily as stir. Gadgets like an electric blender, particularly for frozen cocktails, and low-tech items such as a measuring cup, lemon squeezer, glass jug and punch bowl are also an asset.

Specific glasses, including heatproof models, are ideal but not essential for serving a wide choice of drinks (see also pages 140–1). Apart from practicalities – a long drink can't be served in a short glass – the visual element is also important. There's nothing as elegant or sophisticated as a Martini glass, and a Dry Martini is automatically degraded if served in anything else.

There are three essential steps to preparing a cocktail: shaking, stirring or building. A cocktail shaker needs to be half-full of ice before the ingredients are added, while several ice cubes are required in a stirring or mixing glass, or jug. Some cocktails require a preparatory stage known as muddling. This entails using a muddler, or the back of a spoon, to break down and incorporate ingredients. Salting the rim of a glass, for cocktails such as the Margarita, only requires wiping

the rim with a wedge of lemon and dipping the rim into a saucer of salt. A sharp knife or zester facilitates the preparation of garnishes, which can then be lowered into position using cocktail sticks.

Once you're familiar with the principles of making a cocktail, it's time to experiment and adapt recipes to suit your own taste. After all, that's how many cocktails were devised – by developing a combination that had already been prepared by someone else.

Cocktails are all about style and indulgence, which can easily lead to excess. That's why one chapter of this book is dedicated to the hangover preventions and cures practised in various countries. It's a chapter I kept going back to.

sparkling wines

Does it really have to be champagne for a celebration? Yes, it does. Of course, there are plenty of great alternatives with a similar sparkle, but the nature of a celebration means that it's judged by how it's celebrated. And as we've believed in champagne as the ultimate for so long, anything else seems like a compromise.

While French expertise has elevated champagne production to a fine art, it was the ancient Romans who first established vineyards in the Champagne region of France. But it wasn't until the 17th century, once production methods had become more sophisticated, that champagne became acceptable among the aristocracy. A formative influence in the gentrification process was Dom Pierre Pérignon, a Benedictine monk. Often credited with 'inventing' champagne's effervescence, his real contribution was blending wines. By selecting different grape varieties from various vineyards in the region, he produced wines of greater quality and character. A tribute to his genius is Cuvée Dom Pérignon, a champagne that defines finesse.

Grape picking in Champagne normally begins in September. After the first fermentation, the grape juice, or must, is blended with other still wines, which can be from different vineyards and years. This forms the *cuvée*, or blend, with *cuvées*

usually combining the three principal grape varieties cultivated in Champagne: chardonnay, pinot noir and pinot meunier. Yeast and a little cane sugar are then added, facilitating the second fermentation, which takes place in the bottle. This is the méthode champenoise that produces the bubbles. Non-vintage champagne is generally aged for at least two years, while vintage champagne, made with the wines of a single outstanding year, for at least three years.

Champagnes come in a wide range of blends and styles — from fruit flavours to full-bodied, yeasty, toasty characteristics — reflecting the ratio of each grape variety within the cuvée. Chardonnay provides elegance, pinot noir structure, longevity and depth of flavour, and pinot meunier a perfumed, fruity, spicy character. Blanc de Blancs champagne is made entirely from chardonnay, resulting in an elegant, sophisticated style. Blanc des Noirs champagne is fuller bodied and fruity, and made from either pinot noir or pinot meunier, or a combination of both.

The French love of champagne is fostered from an early age. It's served at baptism celebrations, when adults aren't the only ones to get a taste — a drop of champagne is often placed on the baby's tongue to celebrate the absolution of original sin and entering a state of grace. While renowned as an aperitif, champagne is rarely considered as an accompaniment to food, although, as the French have always known, champagne partners various dishes very successfully. The golden rule is to 'build' throughout a meal by serving progressively fuller-bodied styles, as exemplified during the formal dinner served on 22 January — the feast day of St Vincent, the patron saint of vine growers.

Le Cochelet — a party marking the completion of the harvest — is another annual highlight in Champagne when employers serve a last supper to their grape-pickers. The evening includes a final visit to the wine presses to sample new wines from the casks, while the menu is a hearty line-up of regional dishes. Christmas Eve is when many French families, particularly those in Champagne, bring out the magnums. But then large quantities are necessary to accompany the festive dinner of such favourites as oysters, smoked salmon, *boudin blanc*, capon, venison and foie gras, not to mention ballotine of pheasant or wild boar.

Sparkling wine also assumes a celebratory role in various other countries. An Italian Christmas tradition is to serve asti spumante with panettone — a rich cake made with raisins and candied peel — which is such a good combination that it has inevitably become a year-round event. Asti spumante makes the most of the muscat grape, which has always been prized for its sweetness, even by the ancient Romans. Although poor examples of asti spumante are now icons of kitsch, quality specimens are gorgeous, with vibrant fruit flavours, creamy mousse and balanced, refreshing acidity. Italian sparkling wines, including asti spumante, are also served with panettone at midnight on New Year's Eve. This dessert follows a traditional dinner of either *zampone* (spicy pork stuffed in a pig's trotter), or *cotechino* (pork sausage).

The Spanish ensure good luck in the New Year with a tradition known as *uvas de la suerte* (grapes of good fortune). The first chime at midnight from Puerta del Sol in Madrid, which is broadcast on television and radio, is the sign to begin. A grape must be chewed and swallowed before each subsequent chime. In the interests of fair play, everyone is allotted similarly sized grapes, while young children and grandparents are allowed peeled ones. As the criterion for inclusion is merely a set of teeth, even babies qualify, and are given skinned, de-seeded grape segments. Peeled or not, it's a struggle to swallow the grapes, particularly as laughter inevitably erupts. Once the grapes are finished, the second part of the celebration begins, when children are served non-alcholic cider, the adults cava, to toast the New Year. In classic Spanish style, all-night partying ensues.

Cava, literally 'cellar', is produced with the méthode champenoise. It was first developed in 1872 by Codorniu, after the proprietor, José Raventos, had witnessed how exuberantly champagne was being drunk across Europe. Although cava is produced in various Spanish regions, most comes from Catalonia. The grapes used include parellada for subtle floral aromas and balanced acidity, xarel-lo for velvety freshness, strength and finish, and macabeo for elegant, rich aromas and subtle fruit flavours.

Szampanskoye is Russian sparkling wine, some of which is produced using the méthode champenoise, as well as the same grape varieties used for champagne. Either szampanskoye or champagne provides the New Year's toast in Russia. This actually comprises two toasts: one proposed just before midnight to the year that has passed, and a second in honour of the New Year, timed at the twelfth chime of the Kremlin clock.

The Hungarians like to mix sparkling wine with red wine. Peszgo, literally 'bubbling', means 'sparkling wine', and is produced from various grapes, including indigenous varieties such as harslevelu. Pouring sparkling wine over a strawberry or grape is traditional in the Czech Republic. Devotees say this makes the wine even smoother, rounder and longer, and there's the fruit to look forward to afterwards. Similarly, Austrians serve sekt (sparkling wine) with a bowl of strawberries.

New World wine-makers have had an enormous impact on sparkling wine production, with California, Australia, New Zealand and others taking the classic recipe of pinot noir, pinot meunier and chardonnay, not to mention the méthode champenoise, as a starting point to produce sensational wines. Peach is the preferred fruit-flavour to mix with sparkling wine in Australia, exemplified by a popular cocktail of peach schnapps and sparkling wine. (This is a variation of the Bellini, a classic champagne cocktail made with peach purée, created by Arrigo Cipriani at Harry's Bar in Venice during the 1940s.)

The alluring colour of rosé champagne and sparkling wine, ranging from subtle pinks to deep salmon and coral, has inevitably made them a romantic accessory. But this style can also provide a sublime experience, with complex aromas and flavours spanning strawberries, raspberries, blackberries, morello cherries and blackcurrants. But if rosé can sparkle, then why shouldn't red wine? After all, the qualities of popular red grape varieties, including cabernet sauvignon and shiraz (syrah), taste just as good when bubbly. The best examples of sparkling reds – a speciality of Australia – are rich, velvety and perfectly balanced, with flavours ranging from spicy fruits to cherries with aromas of mulberry, truffles, cedar and chocolate. Fabulous. Sparkling red is versatile enough to be a great aperitif, while also performing a balancing act with food. As a traditional accompaniment to Christmas Day lunch in Australia, it can handle turkey and all the trimmings, as well as plum pudding, with consummate ease.

champagne cocktail

White sugar lump or cube
Dash of Angostura bitters
2 tsp brandy
Champagne, chilled, to top up

Place the sugar lump or cube in a
champagne flute then coat it with a dash
of Angostura bitters. Add the brandy and
gently pour in the champagne.

axis kiss

Dash of Amaretto almond liqueur
Dash of crème de cassis
  (blackcurrant liqueur)
Champagne, chilled, to top up

Into a champagne flute, pour the Amaretto and crème de cassis – the larger the dash, the sweeter the drink – then gently add the champagne.

bellini

25ml (5 tsp) puréed peaches
1 tsp crème de pêche (peach liqueur)
2 dashes of peach bitters
Champagne, chilled, to top up

Pour the peach purée into a champagne flute, then add the peach liqueur and two dashes of peach bitters. Gently top up with champagne.

champanska

100ml champagne, chilled
25ml (1½ tbsp) Smirnoff Black vodka,
  or other premium grain vodka
25ml (1½ tbsp) lime cordial
Garnish: twist of lime

Gently pour the champagne into a flute. In a separate glass, stir the vodka and lime cordial together, then add them to the champagne. Garnish with a twist of lime.

château cardillo

25ml (1½ tbsp) pear juice
Dash of Chambord black raspberry liqueur
Champagne, chilled, to top up

Pour the pear juice into a champagne flute and add the Chambord. Gently top up with champagne.

dorchester coupe
aux fraises

(Serves 4)
For the fruit mixture:
100ml brandy
100ml Grand Marnier orange liqueur
6 fresh strawberries, sliced
2 tbsp caster sugar
Small cinnamon stick
For serving:
100ml dry white wine
400ml champagne, chilled
Garnish: strawberries and sprigs
  of fresh mint

Pour the brandy and Grand Marnier into a glass jar and add the sliced strawberries, sugar and cinnamon stick. Stir briefly, then seal and refrigerate for a day or two.

To serve, stir the fruit mixture and place 1 tbsp of the mixture in each champagne flute. Pour 25ml (1½ tbsp) white wine into each flute, then top up gently with champagne. Add one or two strawberries and garnish with a scattering of mint leaves.

french 75

Ice cubes for shaker
25ml (1½ tbsp) Tanqueray gin,
  or other premium overproof gin
Juice of ½ lemon
2 tsp sugar syrup
Champagne, chilled, to top up
Garnish: slice of lemon

Into a shaker half-full with ice cubes, pour the gin, lemon juice and sugar syrup and shake. Strain the mixture into a champagne flute and gently top up with champagne. Garnish with a slice of lemon.

strawberry flapper

(Serves 2)

8 fresh strawberries, hulled

4 dashes of crème de cassis
   (blackcurrant liqueur)

10 ice cubes

Champagne, chilled, to top up

Place the strawberries in a blender
and whizz briefly, then add the
blackcurrant liqueur and the ice
cubes and continue blending
until smooth.

   Half-fill two champagne flutes with
the mixture, then top up with champagne.

pink panther

20ml (1½ tbsp) Grand Marnier
   orange liqueur
15ml (1 tbsp) crème de fraise
   (strawberry liqueur)
20ml (1½ tbsp) orange juice
20ml (1½ tbsp) grapefruit juice
Champagne, chilled, to top up
Garnish: strawberry and sprig of fresh mint

Into a shaker half-full with ice, pour the
Grand Marnier, crème de fraise and orange
and grapefruit juices, then shake. Strain
into a flute and top up with champagne.
Add a strawberry and garnish with mint.

rising sun

*Fortified by Grand Marnier or Cointreau, this
is a more 'orangey' version of a Buck's Fizz.*

20ml (1½ tbsp) Grand Marnier or Cointreau
   orange liqueur
20ml (1½ tbsp) orange juice
Champagne, chilled, to top up
Garnish: slice of orange

Pour the Grand Marnier or Cointreau into a
flute, add the orange juice then top up with
champagne. Garnish with a slice of orange.

sterling silver

A few ice cubes
125ml champagne, chilled
25ml (5 tsp) Tanqueray vodka,
   or other premium grain vodka
25ml (5 tsp) crème de mure (mulberry
   liqueur)
25ml (5 tsp) pear nectar
Garnish: a few raspberries and
   a twist of orange

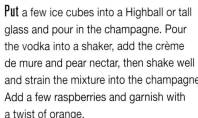

Put a few ice cubes into a Highball or tall
glass and pour in the champagne. Pour
the vodka into a shaker, add the crème
de mure and pear nectar, then shake well
and strain the mixture into the champagne.
Add a few raspberries and garnish with
a twist of orange.

sparkling wines

*The traditional saucer-shaped glass may seem more romantic
but a flute channels the aromas and flavours of champagne and
sparkling wines much better and keeps the mousse going for longer.*

left: *strawberry flapper* **above right:** *sterling silver*

vodka

Mixing readily with numerous partners, vodka soars on its reputation as the most sociable of all spirits. Ironically, this ability to mix has also encouraged the notion that 'all vodkas taste the same'. But they don't. British vodkas, for example, are deliberately neutral spirits, with no aroma or flavour. And as there's no point in drinking a glass of neutrality, these vodkas play a supporting role by providing alcohol that doesn't interfere with the flavour of a cocktail or a mixer.

There are two other distinct types of vodka, which reflect the ingredients used: Scandinavian, which has character, and Eastern European, which has flavour. In Sweden and Finland, this means wheat or barley; in Russia, wheat; in Poland, rye or potatoes. The fresh wheat flavours of Sibirskaya from Siberia, for instance, open up with hints of aniseed and liquorice, while the mellow sweetness of rye is clear in Wyborowa. Potatoes also yield subtly sweet vodkas, such as Luksusowa and Cracovia, with hints of creamy mashed potatoes.

There's no need to add anything to vodkas that have character or flavour — except the right temperature. Scandinavians and Russians typically serve vodka ice-cold, often in chilled glasses. An exception is the Finnish custom of drinking

Koskenkorva with sparkling mineral water. Known as kossurisst, this combination stems from legalities rather than tradition; until 1974 Koskenkorva could only be sold in bars and restaurants mixed with a soft drink.

A Russian belief that vodka fumes promoted drunkenness was one of the reasons behind the tradition of shooting vodka down in one. The Scandinavians are also shooters, while the Poles have a tendency to sip as often as they shoot, which is obviously the best way to enjoy the flavour. Poles also serve vodka at room temperature, enabling more complex styles to reveal their full range of aromas and flavours.

The Polish toast 'na zdrowie', or 'nazdorovye' in Russian ('to your health'), is much more than a polite gesture. Vodka is renowned for its purity, and contains a lower level of congeners – the impurities responsible for hangovers – than other spirits. While devotees claim that drinking vodka is a guarantee against hangovers, this remains a secondary consideration to the quantity consumed, particularly as an enthusiastic refrain in Poland and Russia is 'do dna' ('drink to the bottom of the glass').

A Russian party actually entails a series of toasts because vodka is only drunk after a toast is proposed. A classic opener with family or friends is 'so svidaniyem' ('nice to see you again'). The success of a party rests on the ability of a host or hostess to keep the toasts going: to wealth, romance, beauty, the guests and so on. Arriving late at a party incurs a penalty rather than a toast, although the result is much the same: a full glass of vodka downed in one. With penalties like that, why worry about punctuality?

'Kippis', which is Finnish for 'cheers', is supplemented by 'pohanmaan kautta' ('bottoms up'), while a toast reserved for foreigners is 'holkyn kolkyn'. It sounds intriguing, but doesn't actually mean anything; hearing foreigners mispronounce the toast appeals to the local sense of humour. Nevertheless, proposing a toast in Finland is governed by strict etiquette. The glass must be raised so the arm is horizontal from the shoulder to the elbow. Direct eye contact with each person then follows, the vodka is drunk, and the arm is returned to the raised position. After another round of eye contact, the procedure concludes with a small nod to fellow drinkers.

Even in Eastern Europe, high-strength vodka – way beyond the usual 37.5 to 40 per cent abv – is only drunk neat in desperate circumstances, typically on a park bench. It's used mainly for cocktails and punches. Krepkaya from Russia certainly reinforces a cocktail, with 56 per cent abv, but it provides more than just alcohol. It has a full-bodied, grainy flavour and fruity, apple-and-pear notes that incorporate only a light burn, which is a sign of real quality at this strength.

Ascending the scale, Polish Pure Spirit offers the choice of 57 and 79 per cent abv. If that's still not enough, there is one final option: Spirytus Rektyfikowany – Rectified Spirit – which hits 95 per cent abv. Always warmly received at Polish parties, a favourite combination is equal parts Rectified Spirit and cherry cordial, resulting in Wisniowka. An alternative is Karmelowka which involves caramelizing vanilla-flavoured sugar, seasoning it with salt, then diluting with boiling water. Once the syrup has cooled, it is combined with an equal part of Rectified Spirit. Both Wisniowka and Karmelowka are prepared two to three days in advance, allowing the flavours to integrate.

Vodka has been flavoured ever since it was first distilled; during the 19th-century heyday, more than 100 styles were available in Poland and Russia. Commercial production in both countries dates from the Middle Ages, and was originally a preserve of the aristocracy. Nevertheless, early distillation methods were crude, and it was impossible to rectify, or purify, the spirit. This meant vodka with compromising flavours and aromas. The only solution was to add distractions such as aromatic oils, fruit, herbs and spices, and sweeten it with honey. As the quality of vodka improved, with rectification introduced during the 19th century, flavourings were added for their own merits. One of the most unusual flavoured styles traditionally prepared in Poland, as well as Russia and Sweden, is Zmijowka. Essential at any party during the 16th century, this involved macerating a viper in vodka for several weeks. If the viper was alive at the time of bottling, the flavour was supposedly improved. Renowned as an aperitif and digestif, viper vodka was also prescribed for aches and pains. Sadly, it is not produced commercially, but I once discovered a bottle prepared in the traditional manner using Stolichnaya in a Russian bar. Sensational. With its lightly spicy, meaty flavour, this certainly makes the most of any viper.

Also dating from the 16th century is Zubrowka, which bears the subtitle Bison Brand and a bison on its label. However, no part of the beast flavours this vodka; its name stems from bison grass, a wild herb eaten by European bison roaming the Bialowieza Forest in eastern Poland. Macerating the grass yields grass and hay aromas, while thyme and lavender flavours are balanced by lemon and tobacco.

In Russia, Poland and Sweden, vodka is always accompanied by food, and this doesn't mean a random platter of whatever's available. On the contrary. A specific range of specialities is served, all of which genuinely interact with vodka. Caviar and blinis with soured cream are elite examples in Russia and Poland, while day-to-day fare comprises pickled cucumbers and mushrooms, salted herring fillets with onion and soured cream, ham, sausages, curd cheese and rye bread. Scandinavian favourites go beyond herring to salted roe, gravadlax and crayfish. Tradition stipulates that every time the claws of a crayfish are removed, a glass of vodka should also disappear – down in one. Vodka is often drunk for the duration of a meal, but the remedy for any over-indulgence can be more vodka rather than abstention. Gnesnania Boonekamp, a Polish bitters-style vodka, is all that's required to warm the alimentary canal and, so the theory goes, relieve indigestion.

Other digestif vodkas offer an alternative range of flavours. Goldwasser, originating from 16th-century Gdansk, is flavoured with gypsy rose, valerian root, sandalwood and rosewood, infused in anise-flavoured spirit. This is then redistilled before 23-carat gold leaf is added, originally for its alleged medicinal benefits. Whether this Midas touch contributes to the flavour in any way is debatable. Even if it doesn't, there's plenty to enjoy, with flavours spanning aniseed, liquorice and cooked fruit, culminating in an elegant, dry and sustained finish.

There's a classic Russian saying that states vodka is only drunk for a reason, and if you have a bottle of vodka, then you'll always find a reason. With the comprehensive range of vodkas available, from clear styles offering flavour and character to flavoured and aged specialities, what other reason do you need?

balalaika

Ice cubes for shaker
50ml (3½ tbsp) vodka
15ml (1 tbsp) Cointreau orange liqueur
25ml (1½ tbsp) lime juice

Into a shaker half-full with ice cubes, pour the vodka, Cointreau and lime juice and shake well. Strain the cocktail into a Martini glass.

bison sour

Ice cubes for shaker
50ml (3½ tbsp) Zubrowka Polish vodka
25ml (1½ tbsp) lemon juice
1 tsp sugar syrup
Dash of orange bitters

Into a shaker half-full with ice cubes, pour the vodka, lemon juice and sugar syrup, then add a dash of orange bitters. Shake then strain the drink into a cocktail glass.

caipiroska

3–4 wedges of lime
1–2 tsp sugar syrup
40ml (2½ tbsp) Finlandia vodka,
    or other premium grain vodka
A handful of crushed ice

Place the lime in an Old Fashioned glass or tumbler and pour over the sugar syrup, then break down the lime in the syrup with a muddler or the back of a spoon. Add the vodka and stir in the crushed ice.

cosmopolitan

Ice cubes for shaker
40ml (2½ tbsp) lemon or clear vodka
20ml (1½ tbsp) Cointreau orange liqueur
30ml (2 tbsp) cranberry juice
Juice of ½ lime
Dash of orange bitters
Wedge of orange

Into a shaker half-full with ice, pour the vodka, Cointreau and cranberry and lime juices, then add a dash of orange bitters. Shake then strain into a Highball or tall glass. Before serving, squeeze in the juice from the orange wedge.

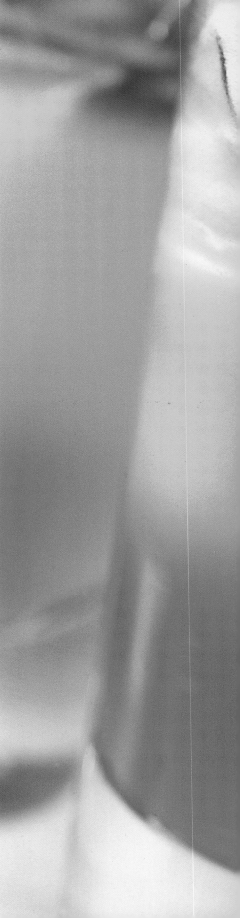

mirage

Several ice cubes
40ml (2½ tbsp) lime juice
40ml (2½ tbsp) Midori melon liqueur
70ml (5 tbsp) non-alcoholic ginger beer
40ml (2½ tbsp) vodka
½ tbsp crème de fraise (strawberry liqueur)

Place a few ice cubes in a Highball or tall glass, then add the lime juice, Midori and ginger beer. Put a few ice cubes into a separate glass and mix in the vodka and strawberry liqueur. Gently 'float' the flavoured vodka onto the ginger beer mixture by pouring it over the front (inward-curving side) of a teaspoon so that they do not combine.

cranberry fields

1 tbsp cranberries, plus extra for garnish
40ml (2½ tbsp) Finlandia cranberry vodka,
    or other cranberry vodka
½ tbsp clear honey
A handful of crushed ice
Garnish: strip of lime zest

In an Old Fashioned glass or tumbler, break down the cranberries with a muddler or the back of a spoon, then add the vodka and honey. Stir, top up with crushed ice, then garnish with a few cranberries and the zest.

above: mirage *right: cranberry fields*

moscow mule

A few ice cubes
50ml (3½ tbsp) vodka
15ml (1 tbsp) lime juice
Non-alcoholic ginger beer, to top up
Garnish: wedge of lime

Put a few ice cubes into a Highball or tall
glass, then add the vodka and lime juice.
Top up with ginger beer and garnish with
a wedge of lime.

sea breeze

Ice cubes for shaker
50ml (3½ tbsp) vodka
100ml cranberry juice
40ml (2½ tbsp) yellow grapefruit juice

Into a shaker half-full with ice cubes, pour the vodka and cranberry and grapefruit juices. Shake to create the 'breeze', or froth. Strain into a Highball or tall glass.

white russian

25ml (5 tsp) vodka
25ml (5 tsp) Kahlua coffee liqueur
Dash of double cream

Pour the vodka and Kahlua into a mixing glass and stir, then pour the mixture into a Martini glass. Gently 'float' the cream onto the flavoured vodka so that they do not mix, by pouring it onto the front (inward-curving side) of a spoon.

To flavour your own vodka, macerate fruit, herbs or spices, or any combination, in a vodka of at least 40 per cent abv.

WOO WOO

Ice cubes for shaker
Wedge of lime
50ml (3½ tbsp) vodka
10ml (½ tbsp) peach schnapps
100ml cranberry juice

In a shaker half-full with ice, place the lime wedge then pour in the vodka, peach schnapps and cranberry juice. Shake, then strain into an Old Fashioned glass or tumbler.

gin

An utterly English institution, gin and tonic is also the perfect example of a classic double act, just like Fortnum and Mason, Gilbert and Sullivan, or the Rose and Crown. But it was Holland, or maybe Belgium, that was the source of a prototype gin called genever – a rye spirit flavoured with juniper. Rather than being a social drink, genever was taken for unsociable ailments such as gout and gall stones. Its ultimate origin may have been the work of north Italian monks, who began macerating juniper in alcohol for medicinal purposes around the tenth century.

Where and when the English first tasted genever is more certain: Holland, in 1585, when English mercenaries arrived to help the Dutch fight Philip II of Spain. A gulp of genever just before battle inspired a false sense of bravery, hence 'Dutch courage'. Enjoying the flavour as well as the effect, surviving mercenaries took the concept back home, and juniper-flavoured spirit went into production, with one minor amendment: a spelling mistake, resulting in 'geneva'.

When William III ascended the British throne in 1689, he boosted sales of domestic spirits such as genever by raising the duty on French brandy – an economic attack reflecting the fact that his country was at war with France.

The king also gave everyone in England the right to distil spirits. Geneva then began to develop its own identity, and its name was abbreviated to gin. Production and consumption went berserk, especially among the working classes. Its appeal? An 18th-century advertising slogan from a London tavern said it all: 'Drunk for a penny, dead drunk for tuppence.'

A series of legal measures in the early 18th century failed to bring epidemic levels of gin consumption under control. It wasn't until 1742 that more successful reforms established the foundations of a modern gin industry. Gin also began to transcend its working-class origins, and was moving in more exclusive circles by the mid-19th century. Being socially acceptable is, of course, entirely a matter of good taste, which made quality control and production methods more pressing issues.

Neutral grain spirit, typically prepared from corn, is at the heart of gin, with the spirit redistilled in the presence of various flavourings known as botanicals, using either of two methods. Steeping involves a period of maceration prior to distilling, with the botanicals and spirit placed in the base of the still. Maceration can be an overnight process, or even longer, helping to release essential oils. Some distillers prefer to place the botanicals in the still just before distillation begins. Alternatively, racking sees the botanicals placed in metal baskets, or trays, in the neck of the still. As the spirit is heated and vapour rises, it acquires essential oils from the botanicals.

Every distiller has a secret recipe which usually comprises six to ten botanicals. The one essential ingredient is juniper; in fact, the legalities are such that gin could be produced using only juniper. Coriander is every distiller's second choice, contributing citrus notes, which are actually more supple than citrus ingredients. Distillers complete the botanical line-up with a supporting cast that includes angelica, ginger, nutmeg, lemon and orange peel, orris root, almonds, cassia bark, cinnamon and grains of paradise. For a spicy, peppery aroma, together with lemony pine flavours, distillers add cubeb berries – the unripe fruit of the Indonesian tailed pepper. Freshness is achieved courtesy of liquorice root – Chinese is the best – while Spanish bitter almonds contribute a nutty flavour.

More botanicals do not necessarily result in a more impressive gin. Balancing the individual characteristics of the botanicals is what makes a gin more enjoyable. For example, angelica's musky, sweet pine aroma is not as significant as its ability to unite the flavours of other botanicals; nutmeg's sweetness and lightly bitter undertone also help to blend other spices, while orris root adds earthiness and sweet violets, which enable other botanicals to assert themselves more forcefully. The alcoholic strength of the gin is crucial in the impact of the botanicals: the stronger the gin, the more intense the flavour. Plymouth gin has a 57 per cent abv version, which releases an initial wave of juniper and coriander, followed by orange and lemon, before the root botanicals – orris and angelica – make an appearance. A refreshing aftertaste brings you back to juniper and coriander. What a gin! Another established method of investing gin with extra flavour is by macerating sloes. This practice evolved in the West Country of England where they are abundant. Topping up sloe gin with bitter lemon is the local practice, giving a drink called a Long Peddler.

While gin has developed a comprehensive repertoire of long drinks and cocktails, its most frequent role is in gin and tonic, or G&T to its friends. This combination has gone in and out of fashion, from icon to cliché and back again. But now it's back in a big way, and just like the original gin, the G&T also has a medicinal provenance, thanks to quinine. A key ingredient of tonic water, quinine is extracted from the bark of a Peruvian tree called the cinchona. This bark's ability to reduce fevers was well known to

South American natives, and 16th-century Spanish conquistadors found it to be effective against malaria. In colonial India, the British took large doses of quinine to prevent malaria and other fevers, but its intensely bitter, even unpalatable taste, was a problem. However, a squeeze of lime or lemon juice was found to improve matters considerably, with sugar smoothing the jagged edges. It was actually an enjoyable, refreshing combination that soon came to be known as Indian Quinine, or tonic water. The next step was adding gin – by then an acceptable means of refreshment for civilized people – which hastened its conversion to a social drink.

Preparing such a drink became far simpler when J Schweppe and Company Limited of London went into action. A patent taken out in 1858 specified: 'An improved aerated liquid known as quinine tonic water.' Colonial links resulted in the name Indian Tonic Water, a term that became official when Schweppe's applied it to commercially produced quinine water in the 1870s. Colonials returning to England from India continued the ritual of mixing gin with tonic, despite the absence of malaria, and it soon became fashionable. Tonic water no longer contains quinine in significant quantities for any medicinal properties to be claimed, and its sole purpose is to provide an enigmatic bitterness.

While British gin reigns supreme internationally, it doesn't enjoy a total monopoly. Larios, often enjoyed with tonic and cola, has been produced in Spain since 1863. And genever, the 'original' gin, remains a national favourite in the Netherlands and Belgium. Genever is based on a spirit produced from wheat, maize, rye and malted barley, known as malt wine, flavoured with juniper and other herbs and spices. There are three main styles: young genever, old genever and korenwijn. Despite the implication, the difference between young and old is not the degree of ageing but the individual recipes. Old genever follows the original recipe and has a straw rather than clear colour. It is also slightly sweeter and more aromatic than the milder young genever – an innovation of the 20th century, which is fast becoming the most popular style in the Netherlands. Korenwijn, meanwhile, is made of the finest quality grain distillates, aged in oak, which accounts for the pale golden colour and mellow flavour. Bols Corenwijn – different spelling, same product – is matured for three years and bottled in hand-made stone jars. Borrel, the Dutch nickname for genever, is usually drunk as an aperitif. Although historically served at room temperature, a long-established custom is to serve genever chilled in a genever glass, which has a stem and foot, or with ice in a tumbler. Korenwijn is also drunk neat and very cold, with devotees insisting on chilled glasses, which turns the spirit lightly syrupy and creates tiny ice crystals. A Dutch custom, particularly at Sunday lunch, is to place a small amount of caster sugar into a shot glass containing young genever. After drinking the genever, the sugar is eaten with a teaspoon.

Flavoured genevers are made with many different types of fruit; redcurrant is particularly fashionable served over ice. In Belgium, fruit-flavoured genevers essentially date from the 1970s, with new styles, including various herbal examples, constantly being devised. In addition to the range of commercially produced genevers, Belgians also buy clear genever for preparing their own fruit infusions at home, or they add egg yolks to make advocaat (see page 95).

Not many spirits have bars devoted entirely to them, but genever bars took off in Belgium during the 1970s. Many are small-scale venues, accommodating 20 to 30 people at the most, and it's often a case of standing room only, but that seems to suit the steady stream of manual and office workers who pop in for half an hour or so, on their way to and from work. I think I'd prefer to reverse the process, though, and briefly pop into the office en route to a far longer shift in a genever bar.

bronx

Ice cubes for shaker
50ml (3½ tbsp) Plymouth gin, or other
    premium gin
25ml (1½ tbsp) dry vermouth
25ml (1½ tbsp) sweet vermouth
Dash of Angostura bitters
Garnish: cocktail cherry

Into a shaker half-full with ice, pour the gin
and the dry and sweet vermouths, and add
a dash of Angostura bitters. Shake well,
then strain into a cocktail glass. Garnish
with a cocktail cherry.

caruso

A few ice cubes
25ml (1½ tbsp) Gloag's gin, or other
    premium gin
25ml (1½ tbsp) dry vermouth
Dash of green crème de menthe
    (mint liqueur)

Place a few ice cubes in a cocktail
glass, then add the gin and vermouth
and a dash of crème de menthe.
    To create a Caruso Blanco, simply
substitute white crème de menthe
for green.

gin & sin

Ice cubes for shaker
25ml (1½ tbsp) Beefeater gin, or other
    premium gin
25ml (1½ tbsp) lemon juice
25ml (1½ tbsp) orange juice
Dash of grenadine

Into a shaker half-full with ice cubes,
pour the gin and lemon and orange
juices, then add a dash of grenadine
(the larger the dash, the sweeter the
cocktail). Shake well, then strain
into a cocktail glass.

gin fizz

50ml (2½ tbsp) gin
Juice of 1 lemon
1 tsp caster sugar
1 egg white (optional)
A few ice cubes
Soda water, to top up

Into a shaker, pour the gin, lemon juice
and sugar, then add the egg white, if using
– the drink will be frothier if you do. Shake
well. Put a few ice cubes into a Highball or
tall glass and strain the gin mixture over
them, then top up with soda water.

la habana

Ice cubes for shaker, plus extra to serve
25ml (1½ tbsp) gin
25ml (1½ tbsp) apricot brandy
Squeeze of lime juice
A few ice cubes

Into a shaker half-full with ice cubes,
pour the gin and apricot brandy and
add a few drops of lime juice, and shake.
Strain the drink into a cocktail glass
three-quarters-full with ice cubes.

million dollar cocktail

*Like the Singapore Sling, this cocktail
was created at the beginning of the
20th century by Ngiam Tong Boon at
Raffles Hotel in Singapore.*

Ice cubes for shaker
30ml (2 tbsp) gin
5ml (1 tsp) sweet vermouth
5ml (1 tsp) dry vermouth
120ml pineapple juice
Dash of egg white
Dash of Angostura bitters

Into a shaker half-full with ice, pour the gin
and the sweet and dry vermouths. Add the
pineapple juice, then a dash of egg white
and a dash of Angostura bitters. Shake
well to froth up the egg white, then strain
into a Highball or tall glass.

gin

*The range of botanicals used to flavour
gin, including juniper, coriander, lemon and
orange peel, nutmeg and ginger, provides
a perfect launching-pad for various mixers.*

negroni

25–50ml (1½–3½ tbsp) gin
25ml (1½ tbsp) sweet vermouth
25ml (1½ tbsp) Campari
Soda water, chilled, to top up (optional)
Garnish: slices of lemon or orange

Pour the gin into a tall glass, add the
vermouth and Campari, then top up with
soda water if desired. (If soda water is
omitted, serve in a Martini glass.) Garnish
with a slice of lemon or orange.

pink gin

Although now a society favourite, the pink gin was originally devised by the Royal Navy to make Angostura bitters, given to sailors for medicinal reasons, more palatable.

50ml (3½ tbsp) gin, chilled
Dash of Angostura bitters
Tonic water, chilled, to top up (optional)

Chill a cocktail glass. Pour the gin into the chilled glass, then add a dash of Angostura bitters. Top up with tonic water, as desired.

singapore sling

From the legendary Raffles Hotel in Singapore, this distinctive pink cocktail was originally created to woo the ladies. 'Sling' is an Americanism, from the German 'schlingen', meaning to swallow quickly.

Ice cubes for shaker
30ml (2 tbsp) gin
15ml (1 tbsp) cherry brandy
120ml pineapple juice
15ml (1 tbsp) lime juice
5ml (1 tsp) Cointreau orange liqueur
5ml (1 tsp) Benedictine liqueur
10ml (2 tsp) grenadine
Dash of Angostura bitters
Garnish: cocktail cherry and wedge
    of fresh pineapple

Into a shaker half-full with ice, pour the gin, cherry brandy, pineapple and lime juices, Cointreau, Benedictine and grenadine, and add a dash of Angostura bitters. Shake well, then strain into a Highball or tall glass. Garnish with a cocktail cherry and pineapple wedge.

sweet city

A few ice cubes
25ml (1½ tbsp) Bols young genever,
    or other premium genever
25ml (1½ tbsp) red vermouth
25ml (1½ tbsp) apricot brandy
Garnish: strip of orange zest

Place a few ice cubes in a Highball or tall glass, then pour in the genever, red vermouth and apricot brandy. Garnish with a strip of orange zest.

left and above: *negroni* above right: *singapore sling*

tequila

Agave, from which tequila is distilled, traditionally enjoyed divine status among the Aztec Indians as it was believed to be the first plant created by the gods. Aztec legend also relates how the gods struck an agave plant with a bolt of lightning that sliced it open, to reveal that the plant had been cooked and the sap converted into a sweet nectar. Once fermented, this provided an alcoholic drink called pulque, from which tequila is descended.

Pulque was not drunk socially as becoming intoxicated with pulque was hailed as a mystical state that provided a direct line to the gods, particularly the goddess of agave, Mayahuel. However, its divine nature was lost on the Spanish conquistadors, who began colonizing Mexico during the 1520s. They condemned pulque for its earthy flavour and low alcoholic strength, although it was, at least, readily available, unlike Spanish wines and brandy. Consequently, the conquistadors began to distil pulque, which increased its alcoholic strength, at the same time improving the flavour. As pulque from blue agave plants was deemed to produce the finest distillate, production developed around the town of Tequila – hence the name – in the state of Jalisco, where blue agave was most plentiful.

Current regulations stipulate that tequila is produced only from blue agave cultivated in Jalisco, certain neighbouring states and Tamaulipas on the Gulf of Mexico. Harvesting the plant, which takes anything from eight to 12 years to mature, means removing the incredibly tough leaves to reveal the bulbous heart, typically weighing up to 70kg. Known as the *pina*, Spanish for pineapple which it resembles, this is the only part used for distillation. Steam-cooking converts the starch content into sugar, and as the agaves are shredded, the sugars are simultaneously washed from the pulp. The resulting liquid, known as *aguamiel*, or honey-water, is fermented and distilled twice using pot stills.

There are two principal styles of tequila: standard and 100 per cent agave. To produce the latter, all the fermentable sugars must be derived from agave, while standard tequila may include up to 49 per cent of other sugars. The connoisseur's choice is 100 per cent agave tequila, but the plant's earthiness can be such that toning it down with other sugars may, for some palates, be an improvement.

Blanco (white or silver) is the original unaged style of tequila, offering the most intense agave experience. More complex styles typically combine earthy, herbaceous and vegetal notes, enlivened by spices such as cinnamon and nutmeg. Reposado spends two to 11 months in oak barrels, which adds vanilla and caramel notes. Anejo, aged for a minimum of one year, takes this a stage further, balancing vanilla, caramel, honey and dark chocolate notes with spicy, herbaceous, chargrilled vegetal flavours.

While tequila is currently enjoyed by an international audience, interest in the agave spirit mezcal as a 'rustic chic' speciality is growing. An essential difference between the two is that agave *pinas* are steam-cooked to produce tequila, while wood-fired ovens are used for mezcal, lending a smokiness evident in the resulting spirit. Mezcal is produced in several regions, although many of the finest specimens hail from Oaxaca, where a local proverb says it all: 'Para todo mal, mezcal. Para todo bien tambien.' ('For all that ails you, mezcal. And to celebrate all that's good as well.') Sotol follows the same principles as tequila, but uses wild rather than cultivated agave, harvested from the mountainsides of the Chihuahua desert. The flavour is correspondingly drier and earthier than tequila or mezcal.

Sotol and mezcal are typically taken neat, while tequila has a more extensive repertoire – not to mention set of drinking rituals. As it was originally a robust spirit, it was far more palatable with full-bodied accompaniments which made the favourite Mexican combination of salt and lemon a natural choice. This gave rise to the custom of licking a little salt from between the thumb and forefinger, downing the tequila in one, and then sucking a lemon wedge. An alternative routine is to follow a sip of tequila with a sip of

sangrita – tomato juice spiked with lemon and orange juice, honey, chillies, Tabasco, Maggi and Worcestershire sauces and salt (see page 45). It's a terrific combination, particularly as the sweet and sour notes of sangrita were designed to mask the rawness of the alcohol, while emphasizing the agave flavour. However, every tequila drink can only aspire to the definitive status of the Margarita: tequila, lime juice and triple sec – an orange-flavoured liqueur such as Cointreau or Grand Marnier, served in a salt-rimmed glass (see page 42).

A benefit of drinking tequila and mezcal in authentic Mexican style is that both are accompanied by *botanas*, or hors d'oeuvres, from the staples of Mexican cuisine such as guacamole and refried beans to *barbacoa* (barbecued lamb), pig's tongue in vinegar, and mushrooms fried in tomato or garlic sauce. In Oaxaca, mezcal is often served with *sal de gusano*: roasted gusano, ground with salt and chilli. Gusano is the same 'worm' – actually the larva of the mariposa night butterfly – that appears in some brands of mezcal. The reason for this dates from a time when innkeepers were notorious for adulterating spirits. A gusano preserved by the spirit was proof of an appropriate alcoholic strength. Needless to say, 'real men' swallow the worm. The gusano is also credited with aphrodisiac and hallucinogenic powers, elevating the spirit to a transcendent plane. And it's supposed to prevent hangovers!

Among many Mexican festivals in which tequila and mezcal play an essential role is *Dia de los Muertos* – the Day of the Dead – on 1 November. Despite its ominous name, this actually celebrates the lives of deceased relatives, and signifies a brief return of their spirits to the grave and family home. Families assemble offerings for the spirits in the form of the deceased's favourite food and drink, either around a specially prepared family altar at home or at the gravestone. Food was originally intended to help the deceased pass through the nine underground labyrinths leading to their final resting place. This subsequently evolved into a belief that the spirits enjoy the 'essence' of the food and drink, while the living actually consume it. A typical menu includes chicken or turkey cooked in *mole*, an elaborate sauce containing chocolate among 24 other ingredients. Enchilladas and *pan de muerto* (bread of the dead) continue the line-up, with refreshments including tequila and mezcal.

Tequila and mezcal also help to celebrate Independence Day on 16 September, while 8 December – the feast day of the Virgin of the Conception, who is also patron saint of the town of Tequila – is celebrated with a *feria*, or festival. In the highlands of Jalisco, home of several renowned distilleries, a 10-day *feria* leads up to the feast day of the Virgin of Guadalupe on 12 December. Distillery employees hold a candlelit procession through the town, singing religious songs en route to a special mass. After that, there's time for just one more party – the big one in the town square.

Pulque continues to flow in Mexico, offering a herbaceous aroma and sweet, lightly acidic, milky flavour, just as it has for the last 2,000 years. Rich in protein and carbohydrates, and with high levels of iron and minerals such as phosphate, potassium and sodium, pulque also has an alcoholic strength of 5 to 8 per cent abv, which provides a rather inexpensive way of having a good time. Its reputation for imparting physical strength, as well as being an aphrodisiac, adds a certain frisson, but despite all these merits, pulque's popularity is in decline.

Often flavoured with fruit, pulque is available from its own dedicated venue, the *pulqueria*. While the greatest concentration of these is in rural areas of southern Mexico, they are also a feature of Mexico City. This all-male enclave – women are allowed to buy pulque but only from a window – is typically decorated with murals of the owner wearing a sombrero, together with a full complement of rural scenes. Apart from drinking and eating, the reason for going to a *pulqueria* is to hang out with the boys and chat over a game of dice, cards or dominoes.

Pulque production remains the preserve of small-scale operators in the countryside, with *tanacals*, or pulque factories, concentrated around Acapulco, along the border with Guatemala, and in Oaxaca. Traditional methods continue using sap from various species of agave, which are different from those used for tequila and mezcal. Fermentation takes place in wooden tanks and is effected using natural air-borne yeast. As pulque has a short lifespan, it is rarely available beyond Mexico, which is yet another good reason for paying the country a visit.

margarita

Wedge of lemon

Salt, for glass rim

Ice cubes for shaker

50ml (3½ tbsp) blanco
   (white or silver) tequila

15ml (1 tbsp) Cointreau orange liqueur

25ml (2½ tbsp) lime juice

Wipe the lemon over the rim of a
Martini glass to moisten it, then dip
the rim into the salt.

   Into a shaker half-full with ice, pour the
tequila, Cointreau and lime juce and shake.
Strain the cocktail into the glass, being
careful not to dislodge the salt.

golden margarita

Wedge of lemon

Salt, for glass rim

Ice cubes for shaker

50ml (3½ tbsp) José Cuervo Gold tequila,
   or other reposado tequila

25ml (1½ tbsp) Grand Marnier
   orange liqueur

25ml (1½ tbsp) lemon juice

Wipe the lemon wedge over the rim
of a Martini glass to moisten it, then dip
the rim into the salt.

   Into a shaker half-full with ice, pour
the tequila and Grand Marnier and add the
lemon juice. Shake then strain the cocktail
into the prepared glass, without dislodging
the salt on the rim.

pomegranate margarita

Wedge of lemon

Salt, for glass rim

Ice cubes for shaker

20ml (1½ tbsp) pomegranate juice

15ml (1 tbsp) triple sec orange liqueur

30ml (2 tbsp) lime juice

50ml (3½ tbsp) tequila

Wipe the wedge of lemon over the rim
of a Martini glass to moisten it, then dip
the rim into the salt.

   Into a shaker half-full with ice, pour
the pomegranate juice, triple sec orange
liqueur and lime juice, then add the tequila
and shake.

   Strain the cocktail into the prepared
glass, being careful not to dislodge the
salt on the rim.

left: *pomegranate margarita* **above:** *golden margarita* **right:** *midori margarita*

hibiscus margarita

Wedge of lemon
Salt, for glass rim
Ice cubes for shaker
70ml (5 tbsp) Gran Centenario Reposado
   tequila, or other reposado tequila
35ml (2 tbsp) triple sec orange liqueur
35ml (2 tbsp) lime juice
25ml (1½ tbsp) strong, sweetened
   hibiscus tea, cooled

Wipe the lemon over the rim of
a Martini glass to moisten it, then
dip the rim into the salt.
   Into a shaker half-full with ice, pour
the tequila and triple sec, then add the lime
juice and the cooled hibiscus tea. Shake
then strain into the prepared glass, being
careful not to dislodge the salt.

brave bull

*This cocktail combines two of Mexico's
finest liquid assets: tequila and Kahlua.*

A few ice cubes
50ml (3½ tbsp) blanco
   (white or silver) tequila
25ml (1½ tbsp) Kahlua coffee liqueur

Place a few ice cubes in a tumbler
and pour in the tequila, then add the
Kahlua. Swirl the glass gently a few
times before drinking.

harvey floor walker

40ml (2½ tbsp) José Cuervo Gold
   tequila, or other reposado tequila
20ml (1½ tbsp) Bacardi Gold rum,
   or other premium gold rum
15ml (1 tbsp) Bols blue curaçao
   orange liqueur
100ml orange juice, chilled

Pour the tequila into a Highball or tall
glass, then add the rum and the curaçao,
and gently pour in the orange juice.

midori margarita

Wedge of lemon
Salt, for glass rim
Ice cubes for shaker
15ml (1 tbsp) lime juice
30ml (2 tbsp) Midori melon liqueur
30ml (2 tbsp) blanco
   (white or silver) tequila
Garnish: wedge of lime

Chill a Martini glass. Wipe the lemon
over the rim to moisten it, then dip the
rim into the salt.
   Into a shaker half-full with ice, pour
the lime juice, then add the Midori
and tequila. Shake then strain the
cocktail into the prepared glass, without
dislodging the salt on the rim. Garnish
with a wedge of lime.

tequila

Tequila thrives in various versions of the Margarita – the world's most popular cocktail – while the full complement of other Mexican recipes makes the most of tequila's herbaceous, spicy flavours.

sangrita

(Makes 1.5 litres)

1 litre tomato juice

10–20 drops each of Worcestershire,
    Tabasco and Maggi sauces

500ml orange juice

75ml (5 tbsp) clear honey

Juice of ½ lemon and ½ lime

Chopped chilli or onion, to taste

Salt and freshly ground black pepper

To accompany: tequila, lightly chilled

Pour the tomato juice into a large mixing
bowl or jug, then add the sauces, orange
juice, honey, lemon and lime juices, and
chilli or onion. Stir well and season with
salt and black pepper to taste.

Cool the drink in the refrigerator for at
least 2 hours before serving. When ready
to drink, serve the tequila and sangrita
strained into separate shot glasses, and
take alternate sips of each.

tequila sunrise

A few ice cubes

25–50ml (1½–3½ tbsp) blanco
    (white or silver) tequila

Orange juice, to top up

2 good dashes of grenadine

Place a few ice cubes in a Highball or tall
glass and pour over the tequila, then top
up with orange juice.

To create the 'sunrise' effect, stand two
straws one against the other in the glass
and pour the grenadine gently along them
so that it settles at the bottom of the glass.
If you prefer, sip the drink through straws.

vampiro

Wedge of lemon (optional)

Salt, for glass rim (optional)

A few ice cubes

50ml (3½ tbsp) blanco
    (white or silver) tequila

Dash of orange or grapefruit juice (optional)

Sangrita, chilled (see recipe above left)

Garnish: slice of lemon

If you prefer, you can serve this drink in
a glass with a salt rim. Simply wipe the
wedge of lemon over the rim of a tall glass
to moisten it, then dip the rim into the salt.

Place a few ice cubes in a tall glass
and pour in the tequila, being careful not
to dislodge the salt. Add the orange or
grapefruit juice, if using, and top up with
sangrita. Garnish with a slice of lemon.

left: *tequila* **far left:** *sangrita* **top left:** *vampiro*

rums

When Christopher Columbus discovered Cuba in 1492, he also found the island to be the perfect habitat for the sugar cane plants he'd brought with him. Thanks to the hot climate, it didn't take long to discover that sugar cane juice left to ferment in the sun yielded an alcoholic drink – the precursor to rum. This was subsequently distilled into something stronger, and sugar cane spirits were produced through-out the region from the early 17th century.

Various names were given to these early rums, including 'sugar wine' and 'kill devil', with 'tafia' adopted by pirates. By the mid-17th century, such euphemisms were replaced by 'rum', which may have been an abbreviation of either of two old English words: rumbullion, meaning strong liquor, or rumbustion, meaning great tumult, or even the Latin for sugar cane, *Saccharum officiarum*.

Rum was initially given to plantation workers as some respite from their appalling living and working conditions, while colonials drank it whenever their stocks of European wines and spirits ran out. A description penned in 1647 summed up the drink: 'It is hot, hellish, and terrible.' The colonials learned to take the edge off rum by serving it as a punch. A Caribbean saying, originally a slave jingle, is an

easy way to remember the recipe: 'One of sour, two of sweet, three of strong and four of weak.' These were lime, sugar, rum and water, respectively, although milk often replaced water, and lemons and mint were favourite extras.

Even in its early days, rum had fervent admirers. Legendary buccaneer Sir Henry Morgan (1635–88) described rum as: 'A friend and brother to one alone in the dark, a warm blanket on a chilly night, an excitement in the cheek, and an inspirer of bold and brave deeds.' The Royal Navy was another core consumer group who used rum as an anaesthetic, but also started giving it to sailors in 1731 as an alternative to beer. By 1740, it was so popular, and so abused, that Admiral Edward Vernon decreed it must be diluted with water. Inadvertently, the admiral contributed to rum's evolving culture. Nicknamed Old Grog, because his cloak was cut from grogram, 'grog' became a standard name for rum with water, as well as a hot rum drink. The word was also length-ened into 'groggy', and applied to sailors who had drunk too much to do anything useful.

By the mid-18th century, rum punch had become fashionable in London society, while the spirit was proclaimed *très chic* in 19th-century Paris when it replaced brandy served after the entrée but before the main course at elaborate dinner parties, to settle the digestion and also rev up the appetite for the remaining courses. During the 1920s, and the dawn of the cocktail era, rum consolidated its allure, and Prohibition in the US resulted in the elite heading for Cuba to enjoy various rum cocktails.

The liberation of Cuba from Spain in 1898 inspired two classic rum combinations: the Cuba Libre (see page 51) and the Daiquiri (see page 51). The former may have been a simple case of victorious allies combining their national specialities: Bacardi rum and American Coca-Cola. The relationship was redis-covered when US servicemen stationed on Trinidad in 1944 mixed their supplies of Coke with the local rum. The following year, The Andrews Sisters spread the message still further with their million-selling record *Rum and Coca-Cola*. The Daiquiri cocktail, meanwhile, was named after Cuba's Daiquiri beach, but it was the American mining engineer Jennings Cox who devised the combination of Bacardi rum and lime juice. After it became a hit with other Americans – and the locals – in Cuba, the Daiquiri went on to conquer the world. Diversification resulted in various fruit-flavoured styles, while the Frozen Daiquiri was created in Havana in 1912, with shaved ice chilling the ingredients and providing a sorbet element.

Rum's versatility in long drinks, cocktails and punches reflects the range of styles available, which in turn reflects the choice of raw materials. Some premium rums are produced from sugar cane juice, released by crushing the canes during the sugar-making process. Agricultural *rhum* comes from *vesou*, the juice obtained directly from machete-cut sugar cane stalks prior to processing. This method dates from the 19th century and is a feature of French colonial rums such as Clément from Martinique. However, many premium rums are also distilled from molasses.

Brands can be blended using rums produced either entirely in pot stills, continuous stills or a combi-nation of both, while also drawing on rums from different countries. Cuban rum is known for its light and delicate, as well as medium-bodied, qualities. Rum from Barbados, Puerto Rico and Trinidad follows suit. Light rums are also produced in Haiti, Jamaica, Guyana and Martinique, alongside richer, more pungent examples with good ageing potential. White rum is a light-bodied, unaged style, generally used as a mixer, although in countries such as Haiti freshly distilled rum, known as clairin, is taken neat. Aged rums are classified as golden (medium-bodied) and dark (full-bodied). In maturing rum, the floral, fruity,

Cognac's superlative status overshadows every other type of brandy, with an abundance of elite styles glorified by de luxe packaging. Louis XIII de Rémy Martin, for example, pours beautifully from its Baccarat crystal decanter. Even if you didn't know that this cognac is a blend of thousands of eaux de vie from the illustrious Grande Champagne appellation – and without knowing what that actually means – the current price tag of around £2,000 for a magnum says it all.

Despite all the glamour, the real action is at the opposite end of the cognac hierarchy, where the terminology is equally unrevealing. There's nothing to indicate that the youngest cognac – VS ('very superior') – is a blend of eaux de vie usually between three and four-and-a-half years old. And what about the other categories such as XO or Napoleon that contain eau de vie at least six-and-a-half years old? Again, price is more revealing – you get what you pay for.

What has always been much clearer is how to drink cognac: neat and with reverence. However, mixing cognac with either tonic or mineral water, not to mention ice, has recently increased its popularity as an aperitif in France. The current consensus is that it's OK to do so with VS, but not with other styles. Meanwhile, cognac has always been mixed in the Far East, where ice, water or cola are typical accompaniments – in China it's even considered an aphrodisiac – while Americans drink it with cola, tonic water or ginger ale.

Mixability of another type has long been established. Blending cognac with grape juice yields the traditional aperitif Pineau des Charentes. Similarly, Floc de Gascon, a blend of armagnac and grape juice, and a speciality of Gascony, is served chilled as an aperitif. Armagnac focuses on the same grape varieties as cognac: ugni blanc, folle blanche and colombard. Cognac, however, is double distilled in pot stills, whereas armagnac is mainly produced using a continuous still, resulting in a more robust, rustic style.

Brandy is as much an overture to an evening as a finale for the Greeks, who drink it neat, often with nuts on the side. However, at midnight on New Year's Eve, Greek brandy accompanies Vassilopitta cake; 1 January is the feast day of Aghios Vassilis, or St Basil, who is the Greek equivalent of Father Christmas. Perhaps the most important ingredient of this rather dense cake, made with olive oil, orange juice and zest, eggs and sugar, is a coin which brings good luck to whoever finds it. The first piece of cake is sliced for the patron saint of the household, or the Virgin Mary, followed by symbolic slices for absent family members. Then everyone present gets a share.

Greek brandy is virtually synonymous with Metaxa although, technically, this is not a brandy. Three varieties of sun-dried grapes – savatiano, sultanina and black corinth – are used to make wines that are subsequently distilled. The characteristic bouquet and sweetness of Metaxa are developed by blending in aged muscat wines. The spirit is then passed through a mixture of botanicals and rose petals.

The muscat grape is also behind the vivacious 'grapey' character of pisco, the national spirit of both Chile and Peru. This explains rival claims: that pisco was first distilled at the beginning of the 18th century in the Elqui valley in Chile as well as in the Ica valley near the Peruvian port of Pisco. At least the countries agree on how to use this brandy – in the pisco sour – although recipes vary. The Chilean version (see page 57) combines pisco, sugar syrup and lime juice with crushed ice. Once poured, it's finished with Angostura bitters and cinnamon, or just cinnamon. The Peruvian version (see page 58) uses the same ingredients, but they are processed in a blender with an egg white, resulting in a frothier drink.

Californian brandies showcase classic European grape varieties, just like the region's wines. Colombard, for instance, which is at the heart of cognac, is a primary choice of Ernest and Julio Gallo, and is blended with other varietals, such as chardonnay and cabernet sauvignon, to give the brandy added roundness and complexity. Meanwhile, pinot noir, chenin blanc and semillon are also used to produce varietal brandies by specialist producers such as Germain Robin.

To get the most from their grapes, European wine-makers have traditionally distilled the pomace – the skins, pips and stalks remaining after the grapes have been pressed. Even the most renowned wine-making regions have a sideline in this style of brandy. Marc de champagne picks up on what champagne-making leaves behind, with some Champagne houses maintaining the tradition of serving marc to grape pickers. While young marc is robust, ageing can refine it into a distinguished digestif. But even aged marc has its detractors, with a local phrase dismissing it as 'fiery enough to make a goat dance'.

Greek wine-makers convert pomace into tsipouro – tsikoudia in Crete – which is often preferred to ouzo. This all-rounder partners coffee during the day, replaces wine with food, and is inevitably accompanied by mezze. A favourite Cretan dish with tsikoudia is a combination of grated tomatoes, olive oil, and *myzithra* (crumbled white cheese), piled onto rounds of dark bread. Just as tsikoudia makes a party, so there is a party to celebrate making tsikoudia. On the day that the village distilleries get going after the grapes have been pressed, there are all-night parties with food and drink, music and dancing.

While many pomace brandies are local favourites, grappa has recently attained international cult status. In addition to its 'rustic chic' appeal, grappa has capitalized on our interest in grape varieties, whether worldwide favourites like chardonnay or local contenders such as nebbiolo. Developments during the 1980s have raised the question, 'When is a grappa not a grappa?' When it's made from whole grapes, but not the stalks, resulting in a softer, fruitier style. This style of grappa is labelled *distillato d'uva*, while *vinaccia* indicates it is pomace-based. Increased and extended use of oak-ageing yields a mellower, more perfumed character, but that's another point of contention between traditionalists, who view this as an erosion of grappa's original character, and progressives, who see it as evolution.

Designer grappa bottles also underline the fact that the contents are increasingly specialized, with chilled grappa now chic among Italy's fashionable set. Meanwhile, grappa's digestif role means it's still served alongside espresso; a favourite variation is to pour grappa into the empty espresso cup to pick up a little warmth and coffee flavour. Grappa's ability to provide instant central heating means that plastic sachets of grappa remain standard issue to the Italian National Guard, to combat cold weather. Biting the sachet is all that's required to release the grappa and raise the temperature.

Fruit brandy has brought various flavours into the limelight, such as raspberry, plum, peach and quince, with Alsace regarded as the source of some of the finest. And if you've ever wondered how a pear gets inside a bottle of poire william, it's all about timing. After the pear tree blossoms in April, the budding fruit is encased in a decanter on the actual tree the following month; the tree looks as though it's growing its own glass. By September, the ripe fruit is joined by pear eau de vie in the bottle.

It's no surprise that Switzerland is renowned for kirsch, as this small country produces the world's largest crop of cherries. Kirsch is distilled from black mountain cherries, the finest of which grow at the top of the tallest trees, while connoisseurs thrill at kirsch made from wild cherries. Served as a digestif, kirsch is also a traditional partner for cheese fondue and is frequently added to the pot as well.

Hungarian fruit brandy, palinka, is served neat as an aperitif, with the toast 'egeszsegedre' ('your health'). The least expensive palinka is alma (apple) which is so cheap that it's considered the drink of the poor. Plums don't fare much better; they're so plentiful that Hungarians refer to them as 'rubbish fruit'. Nevertheless, szilvorium (plum brandy) is a popular digestif, as it is in the Czech Republic, where it's called slivovitz, with cherry, peach and pear also popular styles. Meanwhile, plum brandy is popular with elderly ladies in Japan, where it's sold in cardboard cartons, making it easier to carry home.

A speciality of Normandy, calvados (apple brandy) represents a rustic idyll in a glass. Mature calvados is a digestif, while two-to-three-year-old styles are increasingly drunk on the rocks and in cocktails. While calvados doesn't traditionally accompany food, it's served between courses at formal dinner parties, aiding digestion as well as revving up the appetite for the remaining dishes. Calvados is typically the last drink of the day, but it can also be the first, with *café-calva*, meaning either coffee with calvados on the side, or coffee fortified by calvados. And it's a great way to start the day.

angel's cup

(Makes about 750ml)

½ each of a green apple, pear and
   orange, peeled and trimmed
Small bunch of white grapes
1 apricot, halved and trimmed
1–2 tbsp currants, or to taste
1–2 tsp ground cinnamon, or to taste
1 tsp clear honey
4 tsp caster sugar
Strips of zest from 1 lemon, or to taste
500ml grappa

Place all the ingredients in a large,
sealable carafe or glass jar, and stir
well, then place in the freezer for around
12 hours. Allow to stand a few minutes
at room temperature, then serve in
cocktail glasses.

california kiss

25ml (1½ tbsp) Germain Robin Californian
   brandy, or other premium brandy
75ml (5 tbsp) Galliano liqueur
1 ice cube

Pour the brandy, then the Galliano, into
a cocktail glass. Add the ice cube.

chilean manhattan

*South America meets North America
in this version of the classic Manhattan
cocktail, with pisco replacing bourbon.*

A few ice cubes for mixing
50ml (3½ tbsp) pisco
15ml (1 tbsp) sweet vermouth
Garnish: cocktail cherry

Place the ice in a mixing glass, add the
pisco and the sweet vermouth and stir.
Strain into a cocktail glass, and garnish
with a cocktail cherry.

armagnac daisy

A few ice cubes
60ml (4 tbsp) Janneau VS armagnac,
   or other premium armagnac
Juice of ½ lemon
20ml (1½ tbsp) grenadine
Perrier or other sparkling mineral
   water, to top up

Place a few ice cubes in a tall glass and
pour over the armagnac, then add the
lemon juice and grenadine. Top up with
sparkling mineral water.

chilean pisco sour

Wedge of lemon

Caster sugar, for glass rim,
   plus 1 tsp, or to taste

75ml (5 tbsp) pisco

Ice cubes for shaker

25ml (1½ tbsp) lemon juice

Dash of Angostura bitters (optional)

¼ tsp ground cinnamon (optional)

Wipe the lemon over the rim of a cocktail glass to moisten it, then dip the rim in sugar.

In a small bowl, dissolve 1 tsp sugar in the pisco. Half-fill a shaker with ice cubes, then add the sweetened pisco and the lemon juice.

Shake then strain into the prepared glass, taking care not to dislodge the sugar on the rim. Add a dash of Angostura bitters or ground cinnamon, or both, as you prefer.

left: *armagnac daisy* **background:** *chilean pisco sour*

peruvian pisco sour

75ml (5 tbsp) pisco
25ml (1½ tbsp) sugar syrup
25ml (1½ tbsp) lemon juice
1 tbsp egg white, or to taste

Combine the pisco with the sugar syrup in a small bowl or glass, then transfer to a blender. Add the lemon juice and egg white – the more egg white you use, the frothier the drink will be – and whizz for about 10 seconds. Pour into a cocktail glass.

green moon

Ice cubes for shaker
30ml (2 tbsp) grappa
15ml (1 tbsp) Cointreau orange liqueur
15ml (1 tbsp) lime juice
Garnish: fresh mint leaves

Into a shaker half-full with ice, pour
the grappa, Cointreau and lime juice.
Shake, then strain into a cocktail glass.
Scatter with mint leaves and serve.

olympic cocktail

30ml (2 tbsp) cognac
10ml (½ tbsp) orange curaçao liqueur
80ml (5 tbsp) orange juice

Pour the cognac into a shaker and
add the curaçao and orange juice, then
shake. Strain into an Old Fashioned
glass or tumbler.

flashing fizz

Ice cubes for shaker
50ml (3½ tbsp) kirsch
25ml (1½ tbsp) Lejay crème de cassis,
   or other premium blackcurrant liqueur
Sparkling mineral water, to top up

Into a shaker half-full with ice cubes,
pour the kirsch and crème de cassis.
Shake, then pour into a Highball or tall
glass. Top up with mineral water.

pisco fruit

*While pisco is generally served in the form
of a sour in Chile and Peru, combining it
with fruit juice is a popular option.*

Ice cubes for shaker
100ml pisco
75ml (5 tbsp) fruit juice, such as apple,
   orange or pineapple juice
1 tsp caster sugar, or to taste

Into a shaker half-full with ice cubes,
pour the pisco and fruit juice and shake,
then strain into a cocktail glass. Sprinkle
in some sugar and stir.

st george's fizz

1 white sugar cube
5ml (1 tsp) cognac
5ml (1 tsp) Grand Marnier orange liqueur
5ml (1 tsp) crème de cassis
   (blackcurrant liqueur)
Champagne, chilled, to top up

Place the sugar cube in a champagne
flute and pour on the cognac, Grand
Marnier and crème de cassis. Gently
top up with champagne, and serve.

left: *flashing fizz* far left: *peruvian pisco sour*

Liqueurs

Liqueurs revel in their astonishing diversity of styles, which surpasses every other type of spirit. Flavourings range from herbs and spices to plants and flowers, fruits, chocolate and coffee – not to mention dollops of cream – combined in recipes that can easily exceed 100 ingredients.

Liqueurs were traditionally served as a digestif, a ritual that is now becoming an anachronism. Nevertheless, various brands are facing this situation with a positive attitude, promoting themselves as informal and versatile drinks. On the rocks? Absolutely. With a mixer? You name it. Liqueurs are also riding the current cocktail revival, being an integral element of classic and innovative combinations.

The most historic liqueurs reflect their origins as medicinal elixirs, when herbs and spices infused in alcohol were a state-of-the-art answer to various ailments. Early production was the preserve of monasteries; the Carthusian monks are one order that has remained in the business, at the Grande Chartreuse monastery near Grenoble in France. The world's oldest liqueur, Chartreuse has been produced since 1605, when the monks, renowned for their knowledge of alchemy, were given a recipe for an elixir that supposedly promoted longevity.

Producing Chartreuse remains the monks' sole diversion from a life of silent prayer, with computerized production allowing even more time for their devotions. The recipe is strictly confidential; all that's revealed is that grape-based spirit features in a sequence of distillations, infusions and macerations, involving around 130 different herbs and plants. Of the two styles produced, Green Chartreuse is the more popular, and stronger at 55 per cent abv, yielding dry, spicy flavours and aromas, while yellow Chartreuse at 40 per cent abv is sweeter on the palate with citric, honeyed notes. Both are traditional digestifs, served neat, on the rocks, or with a cup of coffee, although Green is the more versatile. In France, it's popular as a long summer drink with tonic or soda water and ice; in winter, it's added to drinking chocolate, especially after a day's skiing.

In the secular world, Galliano relies on more than 30 herbs, such as star anise and lavender. Its vivid yellow colour and tall, slender bottle – inspired by classical Roman columns – ensure instant recognition. Galliano was named after Major Giuseppe Galliano, an Italian national hero from the Abyssinian Wars in the 1890s. But the associations go beyond the Abyssinian campaign. During the California gold rush, many Italians set sail for America armed with a bottle of Galliano. As the colour resembled a golden nugget, it was elevated into a good-luck mascot, while also acting as a souvenir of home. Galliano's most prominent role is in the Harvey Wallbanger (see page 65). Harvey was a real person – a prize-winning Californian surfer who was fond of Screwdrivers (vodka and orange juice), but personalized them with a drop of Galliano. While celebrating a particular surfing victory, he drank one too many and, on trying to leave the bar, kept banging into the walls with his surfboard. What else could the cocktail be called?

The popularity of the Margarita (see page 42) has always depended on the liqueur content – triple sec. Literally 'triple dry', this refers to orange-flavoured liqueurs such as Cointreau and Grand Marnier. Drawing on the flavour of distilled sweet and bitter orange peels, Cointreau turns opalescent when served neat over ice, and develops a fresh range of aromas such as mint, eucalyptus, nutmeg and cardamom. Grand Marnier – the distilled essence of wild oranges and cognac matured in oak casks – continues its classic digestif role, particularly in Asia. But why wait until after a meal? Italians often enjoy a glass with a dessert of vanilla ice cream and strawberries, which are also drizzled with the liqueur.

Italy's most popular liqueur, however, is Limoncello. Originally a speciality of the Amalfi coast, Limoncello is now produced throughout the country. An infusion of unripe cedro lemons in neutral alcohol extracts essential oils from the zest, prior to the addition of sugar and lemon juice. Traditionally served over ice as a digestif, Limoncello is increasingly mixed with tonic and even spirits such as tequila, while Sicilians enjoy it with panettone at Christmas.

As well as being celebrated for its wines, Burgundy is also home to the blackcurrant, which has been famous since the Middle Ages for its therapeutic and curative properties. Burgundian genius subsequently developed the ultimate blackcurrant liqueur – crème de cassis. Denis Lagoute, a Burgundian master distiller, perfected his formula for crème de cassis in 1841, and the Lejay Lagoute distillery continues his work. Served on ice as a refreshing summer drink, cassis has found its apotheosis in Kir: a dash of cassis in white wine (Kir Royale replaces white wine with champagne). This combination is attributed to Canon Felix Kir, mayor of Dijon after the Second World War, who only served Kir at his receptions.

Chambord's wonderfully rich, smooth and distinguished flavour, based on small black raspberries, is also becoming indispensable as a cocktail ingredient. A current American trend is to combine Chambord with champagne for a variation of the Kir Royale, while Australians prefer Chambord Adrenaline: equal parts Chambord and ice-cold vodka. Chambord dates from the reign of Louis XIV, when it was served to members of the king's hunting parties in the forests surrounding the Château of Chambord, a huge *folie de grandeur* completed in 1685.

Various spirits have recently diversified into liqueurs, with Scotch whisky at the core of Stag's Breath – a light, dry combination with an overtaste of waxy honeycomb. Rum is the starting point for Malibu, while tequila can be transformed into the luscious and earthy digestif Agavero, which also contains damiana, an aphrodisiac herb from Baja California. Although Southern Comfort is often associated with bourbon, it doesn't contain any whiskey. For this sublime creation we have bartender M W Heron to thank. Working in New Orleans during the 1880s, Heron was concerned about selling whiskey of harsh and variable quality, so he blended his own full-bodied, smooth spirit from a secret recipe, which he launched at his new bar on Beale Street in Memphis. On moving to St Louis, he created the St Louis Cocktail: Southern Comfort with a twist of lemon. A sign above the bar read, 'St Louis Cocktail, made with Southern Comfort. Limit of two to a customer (no gentleman would ask for more).'

Although crème and cream liqueurs sound similar, they are different. And while the latter is enjoying peak popularity, the former's heyday was the 19th century. Crème liqueurs are produced by infusing flavourings, such as fruits or chocolate, in a combination of spirit and sugar syrup, and served diluted with water as an aperitif, or neat as a digestif. This convention is now passé, but crème liqueurs remain essential in classic cocktails, such as the Grasshopper (see page 64) and Brandy Alexander. Cream liqueurs were effectively pioneered by Baileys, which was launched in 1974. Combining two of Ireland's finest assets – whiskey and fresh double cream – Baileys can be served straight up, or on the rocks.

While Ireland dominates the cream sector, Amarula is a South African cream liqueur with a fruity-toffee taste derived from the fruit of the marula tree. Known locally as the Marriage Tree, weddings are performed under its branches, and the fruit is prized as an aphrodisiac. Marula fruit must be collected as soon as it ripens, in February, otherwise elephants devour them. The fruits are pulped, fermented and distilled to produce a spirit that is matured in oak for three years prior to blending with fresh cream.

The traditional role of liqueurs as digestifs is exemplified by coffee-flavoured styles. Ideal as an accompaniment to cigars and coffee, or even added to coffee, liqueurs are also essential in digestif cocktails such as the Black Russian. Mexican coffee beans and sugar cane spirit combine in Kahlua, while Jamaican Blue Mountain coffee beans with vanilla and sugar cane spirit comprise Tia Maria. Toussaint coffee liqueur, from Haiti, is named after the soldier and statesman General Toussaint L'Ouverture – a national hero of Haitian independence, declared in 1804. Locals are particularly fond of Papa Toussaint (see page 65) – equal parts Toussaint and dark rum, on the rocks – as a digestif. But, just like other liqueurs, Toussaint is also popular as an aperitif. And that's the whole point of liqueurs. Being right for any time and any occasion, their appeal is timeless and totally 'now'.

france angleterre

A few ice cubes
50ml (3½ tbsp) green Chartreuse
    herbal liqueur
50ml (3½ tbsp) pineapple juice
Dash of gin

Place a few ice cubes in a Highball
or tall glass, then add the Chartreuse
and the pineapple juice. Finish with
a final dash of gin.

frankie

25ml (1½ tbsp) Frangelico hazelnut liqueur
25ml (1½ tbsp) Kahlua coffee liqueur
25ml (1½ tbsp) Baileys Irish Cream
25ml (1½ tbsp) double cream

Pour the Frangelico into a shaker and add
the Kahlua, Baileys and double cream.
Shake then strain into a small wine glass
or a Martini glass.

harakiri

*With a vibrant green colour and
distinctive flavour, Midori, from Japan,
is an indispensable cocktail ingredient.*

30ml (2 tbsp) Midori melon liqueur
30ml (2 tbsp) white rum
30ml (2 tbsp) lemon juice

Pour the Midori into a shot glass or small
tumbler, then add the white rum, followed
by the lemon juice.

grasshopper

Ice cubes for shaker
25ml (1½ tbsp) green crème de menthe
    (mint liqueur)
25ml (1½ tbsp) white crème de cacao
    (chocolate liqueur)
25ml (1½ tbsp) double cream
Garnish: slice of lime or cocktail cherry

Into a shaker half-full with ice, pour the
liqueurs and add the cream. Shake then
strain into a cocktail glass. Garnish with
a slice of lime or a cocktail cherry.

loch almond

25ml (1½ tbsp) Amaretto almond liqueur
25ml (1½ tbsp) blended Scotch whisky
Ginger ale, chilled, to top up
Garnish: thin strip of orange zest

Pour the Amaretto into a Highball or tall
glass and add the Scotch, then top up
with ginger ale. Garnish with a thin strip
of orange zest curled into a spiral.

long, slow, comfortable screw up against the wall

*Galliano appears in a number of cocktails
with equally suggestive names: the
Golden Nipple, for example, combines
Galliano with an Irish cream liqueur.*

A few ice cubes
15ml (1 tbsp) Galliano liqueur
30ml (2 tbsp) vodka
15ml (1 tbsp) sloe gin
15ml (1 tbsp) Southern Comfort
Orange juice, to top up
Garnish: cherry and a slice of orange

Place a few ice cubes in a tall glass
and add the Galliano, vodka, sloe gin
and Southern Comfort. Top up with
orange juice and garnish with a cherry
and a slice of orange.

mudslide

1 banana, peeled
20ml (1½ tbsp) vodka
20ml (1½ tbsp) Kahlua coffee liqueur
20ml (1½ tbsp) Baileys Irish Cream
10ml (2 tsp) crème de banane
    (banana liqueur)

Place the banana in a blender and add
the vodka, Kahlua, Baileys and banana
liqueur. Whizz until blended then pour
into a tall glass.

and Underberg (see page 87) are just as likely to precede beer. As German beer can be served very cold, this practice warms up the stomach beforehand. Norwegians prefer to drink aquavit (see page 93), their national spirit, after beer so that its delicate flavour lingers on the palate.

Although beer is usually drunk neat, there are also opportunities to mix and match. The Portuguese, for instance, enjoy a Tango – a small glass of lager with a few drops of grenadine – as well as Greensands, which refers to equal parts lager and ginger ale. During the Communist era, a popular drink in Czechoslovakia was Magicke Oko (Magic Eye), which comprised a pint of beer with a shot of rum and peppermint liqueur. The advantages of this concoction were that the ingredients were generally available, despite frequent shortages of other items, and it was also a cheap way to have a good time. Czechs no longer order a Magicke Oko, but a shot of rum is still a popular extra in a glass of beer, with beer an all-day, everyday staple, which also rounds off the evening as a digestif.

Poles enjoy beer, but with the national palate used to something much stronger – vodka – it is often fortified by combining equal parts stout and porter with Rectified Spirit; with a strength of 95 per cent abv, Rectified Spirit certainly makes up for the beer. Known as Porterowka, this party favourite is served either cold (see page 71) or warmed as a reviving winter drink (see page 123).

Beer and tequila make a great double-act in a Mexican routine known as The Submarine. A shot glass containing tequila is placed inside an inverted Highball glass, so that the base of the Highball glass 'closes' the top of the shot glass. With the shot glass held in place, the Highball is turned rightways up, leaving the shot glass upside down. The Highball is then filled with Mexican beer, and as the beer is sipped, the movement of the Highball agitates the shot glass, freeing some tequila into the beer. It's a perfect example of a slow-release mechanism, particularly useful when you need to pace yourself.

As an all-occasion drink, beer has forged numerous alliances with food. Guinness traditionally accompanies Irish stew, as well as being one of the ingredients, although its most celebrated partnership is with seafood, particularly oysters. Beer is also popular with crab on the east coast of the US, and it's the German national drink, often replacing wine at mealtimes. While popular with pretzels, beer is compulsory with *bierwurst* sausage, which, despite the name, does not contain any beer; it just means they make a perfect pair. Similarly, in western Austria, beer is drunk in a big way, served with dishes such as offal, steak and chicken.

Tapas are renowned for their partnership with sherry and wine, but the Spanish also serve a specific range with beer: ham, cheese, olives, slices of pork on bread and pork with fried peppers. As well as being an aperitif, beer is often drunk with the main course, and beyond. Although they require some preparation, dried, salted *pevides* (melon seeds) are the preferred Portuguese accompaniment to beer, which accentuates the salty flavour. A less salty but equally popular partner is *tremocos* (beige-coloured beans), which are boiled in salted water. The Portuguese also like to drink beer with grilled sardines for a summer lunch, and with barbecued chicken during winter.

michelada

Wedge of lime
Salt, for glass rim
25ml (1½ tbsp) lime juice
50ml (3½ tbsp) tequila (optional)
Mexican beer or lager, such as
    Corona, Dos Equis Amber or
    Negro Modelo, chilled, to top up

Wipe the wedge of lime over the
rim of a tall glass to moisten it, then
dip the rim into the salt. Pour the
lime juice and tequila, if using, into
the glass, being careful not to dislodge
the salt on the rim, then top up with
beer or lager.

black & tan

English-style bitter beer
Guinness, chilled, to top up

Half-fill a tall glass with bitter beer, then add the Guinness. Leave the drink to settle for a few moments before drinking.

black velvet

Guinness, chilled
Champagne, chilled, to top up

Half-fill a champagne flute with Guinness and leave it to settle for a few moments. Top up with champagne.

lime shandy

Dash of lime cordial
Dash of lemon juice
Equal parts beer and sparkling lemonade, chilled, to top up

In a tall glass, place a dash of lime cordial and some lemon juice. Then top up with equal amounts of beer and lemonade.

original shandy no.1

50ml (3½ tbsp) lemon juice or lime juice
100ml soda water
3 tsp caster sugar
English-style bitter beer, chilled, to top up

Pour the lemon or lime juice into a tall glass, then add the soda water. Add the sugar and stir to dissolve, then top up with bitter.

polizeikontrolle

20ml (4 tsp) Absolut Kurant vodka or other blackcurrant vodka
10ml (2 tsp) blue curaçao orange liqueur
20ml (4 tsp) lemon-flavoured sugar syrup
120ml lager, chilled
80ml sparkling white wine, chilled

Chill a beer glass. Pour in the vodka, add the blue curaçao and lemon syrup and stir. Pour in the lager and stir gently, then add the sparkling white wine. Stir gently before drinking.

porterowka

(Makes 500ml)
250ml Rectified Spirit,
    or any other overproof vodka
125ml stout
125ml porter

Pour the vodka into a large bottle, add the stout and porter and shake gently a few times to combine them. Refrigerate for 2–3 days before serving. Serve cold, in tall glasses.

red eye

Juice of ½ large lemon
30ml (2 tbsp) Worcestershire Sauce
30ml (2 tbsp) vodka
Lager, chilled, to top up

Pour the lemon juice into a Highball or tall glass, add the Worcestershire Sauce and vodka, and stir. Top up with lager.

shandy no.2

25–50ml (1½–3½ tbsp) of either gin, vodka, or tequila, as preferred
25ml (1½ tbsp) lemon juice or lime juice
English-style bitter beer, chilled, to top up

In a tall glass, mix your chosen spirit with the lemon or lime juice. Top up with bitter.

snake bite

This inexpensive and effective partnership has long been a basis for youthful enjoyment in the West Country of England.

Lager or Guinness, chilled
Cider, chilled, to top up

Half-fill a tall glass with lager or Guinness, according to preference, then add the cider. Stir a few times before drinking.

In spite of their numerous idiosyncrasies, whiskies can easily be divided into three categories: local brands which are produced in countries as diverse as Spain, Poland, Korea, Japan, New Zealand, India and Brazil; internationally popular whiskies from Ireland, the US and Canada; and, in a class of its own, Scotch whisky – the world's best-selling international spirit.

Although Scotland has ended up on top, that's not where it all began. Missionary monks brought the knowledge of distillation to Ireland in the sixth century, having learned it from Arabs who distilled flowers and plants to produce perfume. By the 12th century, Irish monks were applying the process to grain, converting surplus barley into a spirit that was believed to have medicinal properties and promote longevity. Scottish farmers soon followed suit.

It was subsequently due to Scottish and Irish settlers that the distillation of whisky evolved in the US and Canada during the 18th century. Irish whiskey (spelled with an 'e') was then the world's top-selling style, an accolade that Scotch whisky acquired at the end of the 19th century. And that's how it's going to stay, particularly as ever more palates are seduced by the qualities of malt whisky.

Malt whisky is distilled from malted barley, which is dried over peat fires to absorb the peat reek, or smokiness, and then double distilled in pot stills. Classified on the basis of geographical origin, Lowland malts are generally the mildest, with Highland malts more aromatic and robust. Islay malts are the most powerful, with smoky, peaty, salt-water and seaweed notes. Speyside malts are considered the finest and most delicate, with almost half of Scotland's distilleries located in the region.

Despite the growing appreciation of malts, around 95 per cent of total production is accounted for by blended whisky. The practice of blending malts with grain whiskies, which have less pronounced characteristics, developed in the 19th century as malts were considered too intense for everyday drinking. But blending is not a dilution. A blend can include between 15 and 50, or even more, malt and grain whiskies of varying ages and from different locations, selected for their ability to complement each other. In Scotland, both blended and malt whisky are taken neat or with a little water, which helps to reveal their character. Blends and lighter malts are popular as aperitifs, while fuller-bodied styles are reserved as digestifs. And in between? Serving malt or blended whisky during a meal is becoming increasingly fashionable. Whisky is an essential partner to that icon of native cuisine, the haggis (highly seasoned sheep offal, onions and oatmeal cooked in a sheep's stomach). An additional dram, or measure of whisky, is sometimes poured over the haggis. Another classic partner is black bun, a rich fruitcake often served at Hogmanay, or New Year's Eve. This is when Scottish tradition extends an open-door policy to visitors, who are expected to arrive either with something to eat, usually black bun, or something to drink, preferably whisky, and a symbolic lump of coal representing warmth. Guests pour the host a wee dram from their bottle, keeping the remainder for subsequent hosts.

Fortunately, the Scots don't have to wait long until the next annual highlight, with Burns Night on 25 January commemorating their national poet, Robert Burns (1759–96). Burns supplemented his meagre income from farming and writing by working as a customs and excise officer, which included collecting taxes from whisky distillers. The Burns Night menu comprises cock-a-leekie soup made from chicken and leeks, haggis, tatties (potatoes) and neeps (swede), followed by a pudding of either trifle flavoured with whisky, or Atholl Brose (oatmeal, honey and whisky). The haggis makes a spectacular entrance, paraded around the dining room accompanied by a few verses from Burns' *Address to the Haggis* and a musical overture from a bagpiper who is traditionally paid with a dram of whisky.

Revered around the world, Scotch whisky has nevertheless been translated into the local drinking culture of various countries. The point of Scotch Rocks, a classic American style, is that melting ice extends the whisky into a slightly longer drink. Ice is also a key element in Japan, where strict etiquette governs how Scotch is served. The spirit is poured into the glass, ice is added, then water, with stirring the final touch. Similarly, preparing a Highball means filling the glass with ice, adding Scotch, and stirring. Thirteen times is stipulated for an ultimate Highball, and who would want to make anything less? But that's not the end of it. More ice is added to compensate for 'meltage', then the drink is ready to receive its quota of soda and a slice of lemon.

In Spain and France, mixing is also the name of the game – twenty- and thirty-somethings typically combine Scotch with cola or lemonade. Spaniards also have the option of mixing a local brand, DYC. This may be the only Spanish whisky, but at least there are two styles to choose from: five- and eight-year-old. Both are blends of malt and grain whiskies, with all the ingredients sourced in Spain, and the entire production process undertaken in Segovia.

Irish whiskey is renowned for combining smoothness and delicacy with complexity, reflecting the fact that it is triple distilled, and that the malted barley is unpeated, thereby avoiding the smokiness characteristic of Scotch. Irish whiskey is usually taken neat or mixed with the same amount of water to bring out the flavour. In an Irish pub, a glass of whiskey is accompanied by a jug of water for do-it-yourself mixing, in accordance with a traditional Irish saying: 'You must never steal another man's wife, and you must never water another man's whiskey.' The point of visiting a pub in Ireland is to socialize and enjoy the art of conversation, which can easily develop into singing. This type of spontaneous fun is defined as the *craic* (pronounced crack), in which Irish whiskey plays an integral role.

Canadian whiskey, which can be produced from either corn, rye, barley or wheat, or indeed any combination of these grains, is renowned for its light, soft, full-bodied flavour. Bourbon is also distilled from the same ingredients in Kentucky, but with another proviso being that a minimum of 51 per cent corn must be used. Both Canadian and bourbon are drunk neat, on the rocks, or with water, although cola is the key mixer throughout the US and Canada. Another classic combination for Canadians is Rye 'n' Dry: Canadian whiskey with ginger ale and a slice of orange.

Bourbon's cocktail repertoire is led by the Manhattan (see page 78), thought to have been invented in New York in 1874 when the future Lady Randolph Churchill, Sir Winston Churchill's mother, hosted a banquet to celebrate the election of Samuel Tilden as governor of New York State. The bartender created a special mixture of bourbon and sweet vermouth to mark the occasion and called it after the club where the celebrations took place: the Manhattan.

Embodying the spirit of the American South is the Mint Julep (see page 76), which has been around, in one form or another, since the early 19th century, but is now an essential feature of the Kentucky Derby. Tradition dictates that a Mint Julep is raised as a toast to the winner of the race known as the Run for the Roses, since the trophy for the winning horse is a garland of red roses. An abundance of fresh mint is always available during Kentucky's spring racing season, particularly as several bourbon distilleries grow mint in their grounds. The question is, how best to incorporate the mint within the Julep? One school of thought insists the leaves are pounded and their juices wrung through a cloth. An opposing faction prefers tender young leaves to remain whole and be muddled in the bottom of a glass. It's a tricky one, as both techniques have their merits. I'll just have to try each one again before making up my mind. And I'm not going to rush into a decision either!

mint julep

Sprig of fresh mint leaves

1 tsp caster sugar, or 2 tsp sugar syrup

2 tsp water

A handful of crushed ice

50ml Maker's Mark bourbon, or other
  premium bourbon

Put the mint into a Highball or tall glass
and add the sugar and water. Break down
the mint with a muddler or the back of a
spoon, then add the crushed ice. Pour
over the bourbon and stir until the glass
is frosted.

bourbon sour

Ice cubes, cracked, for shaker
80–120ml lemon juice
1½ tsp sugar syrup, or ¾ tsp caster sugar
50ml (3½ tbsp) Wild Turkey bourbon,
    or other premium bourbon
Soda water, to top up
Garnish: cocktail cherry, slice of orange

Into a shaker half-full with cracked ice,
pour the lemon juice, sugar syrup and
bourbon and shake well. Strain into a tall
glass and top up with soda water. Garnish
with a cocktail cherry and a slice of orange.

irish rickey

A few ice cubes
50ml (3½ tbsp) Millars Irish whiskey,
    or other premium Irish whiskey
Juice of ½ lime
Sparkling mineral water, to top up

Place a few ice cubes in a Highball or tall
glass, then pour in the Irish whiskey and
add the lime juice. Top up with sparkling
mineral water.

josephine

A few ice cubes
30ml (2 tbsp) soda water
60ml (4 tbsp) Dewar's Scotch whisky,
    or other premium Scotch whisky
30ml (2 tbsp) Mandarine
    Napoleon liqueur
30ml (2 tbsp) orange juice
30ml (2 tbsp) lemon juice
Garnish: twist of orange

Half-fill a Highball or tall glass with ice
and pour over the soda water. Into a shaker,
pour the Scotch, liqueur and orange and
lemon juices, and shake. Strain into the
glass and garnish with a twist of orange.

loretto lemonade

Ice cubes for shaker
40ml (2½ tbsp) Maker's Mark bourbon,
    or other premium bourbon
15ml (1 tbsp) Midori melon liqueur
15ml (1 tbsp) lime juice
75ml (5 tbsp) apple juice
Ginger beer, chilled, to top up

Into a shaker half-full with ice, pour the
bourbon, Midori and lime and apple juices
and shake well. Strain into a Highball or tall
glass and top up with ginger beer.

lynchburg lemonade

Ice cubes for shaker, plus a few ice cubes
50ml (3½ tbsp) bourbon or American
    whiskey
25ml (2½ tbsp) Cointreau orange liqueur
Juice of 1 lemon
15ml (1 tbsp) sugar syrup
Sparkling lemonade, to top up
Garnish: slice of lemon

Into a shaker half-full with ice cubes, pour
the bourbon or whiskey, Cointreau, lemon
juice and sugar syrup, and shake.
    Place a few ice cubes in a Highball
or tall glass, then strain over the flavoured
bourbon or whiskey. Top up with lemonade
and garnish with a slice of lemon.

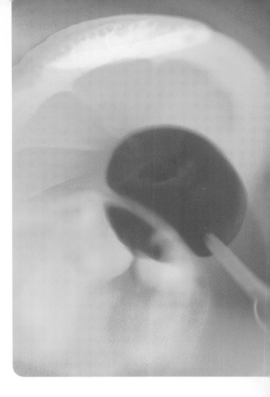

old fashioned

½ white sugar cube
Dash of Angostura bitters
1–2 tbsp water
1 ice cube
50ml (3½ tbsp) bourbon or rye whiskey
Garnish: cocktail cherry and a slice each
    of lemon and orange

Place the sugar in an Old Fashioned glass
or tumbler and drip on a dash of the
Angostura bitters. Add enough water to
cover the sugar, then break it down with
a muddler or the back of a spoon. Add a
single ice cube and pour over the bourbon
or whiskey. Garnish with a cocktail cherry
and a slice each of lemon and orange.

perfect manhattan

A few ice cubes

50ml (3½ tbsp) American or Canadian
   whiskey

25ml (2½ tbsp) dry vermouth

25ml (2½ tbsp) sweet vermouth

Dash of Angostura bitters

Dash of syrup from a jar of cocktail
   cherries

Garnish: twist of lemon or cocktail cherry

Place a few ice cubes in a mixing glass and
add the whiskey, dry and sweet vermouths,
and a dash each of Angostura bitters and
cocktail cherry syrup. Stir well to combine,
then strain into a cocktail glass. Garnish
with a twist of lemon.

   For a dry version of the Perfect
Manhattan, omit the sweet vermouth; for
a sweet version, omit the dry vermouth.
Garnish the sweet version with a cocktail
cherry instead of the lemon.

rob roy

25ml (2½ tbsp) blended Scotch whisky

25ml (2½ tbsp) sweet vermouth

Dash of Angostura bitters

Garnish: cocktail cherry on a stick

Pour the Scotch into a shaker, add the
vermouth and a dash of Angostura bitters,
then shake. Strain into a cocktail glass
and garnish with a cocktail cherry
on a stick.

whiskies

*Different styles of whiskey, including
Scotch, Irish, bourbon and Canadian,
each contribute individual characteristics
to a mixed drink or cocktail.*

southern eggnog

This is a traditional Christmas and New Year drink in much of the US. Guests often present their host with a bottle of bourbon, and preparing the drink becomes the focal point of a party.

(Serves 6)
3 eggs, separated
9 tbsp caster sugar
125ml bourbon
150ml whipping cream
125ml milk
Nutmeg, grated

Whisk the egg whites until stiff but not dry, then gradually add 3 tbsp sugar, whisking continuously. Set aside. In a large serving bowl, beat the egg yolks, then add 3 tbsp sugar and continue beating until well blended. Very slowly add the bourbon to the yolk mixture, beating continuously.

Fold in the whisked egg whites, taking large spoonfuls and blending them into the sweetened egg and bourbon mixture in a gentle figure-of-eight motion to retain as much air from the egg whites as possible.

Whip the cream until it is almost stiff, then gradually add 3 tbsp sugar and continue beating until the cream holds a peak. Gently fold the cream into the egg and bourbon mixture, then gently stir in the milk. Chill for at least 4 hours in the refrigerator. Serve cold, either Kentucky-style in mugs, or in tall glasses, sprinkled with grated nutmeg.

whisky collins

50ml (3½ tbsp) blended Scotch whisky
25ml (2½ tbsp) lemon juice
Dash of sugar syrup
Soda water, chilled, to top up
Garnish: slice of lemon

Pour the Scotch and lemon juice into a shaker, add a dash of sugar syrup and shake. Pour the flavoured whisky into a Highball or tall glass and top up with soda. Garnish with a slice of lemon.

left: *southern eggnog* **above right:** *rob roy*

From Portugal to Egypt, Mediterranean palates are united in their love of aniseed, although each country has its own idiosyncratic examples of aniseed drinks, and evolved different traditions determining exactly how they should be served. A theatrical and typically Italian way to enjoy sambuca is *con la moscha* (with the fly). The flies are represented by roasted coffee beans floating on the surface, but they are more than mere accessories; legend states that having three beans – symbolizing faith, hope and charity – brings good fortune. The serving ritual involves igniting the spirit, marvelling at the effect, then blowing out the flames. Once the sambuca has cooled down, it's drunk and the beans are crunched. Apart from good luck, the beans provide an effective counterpoint to the aniseed flavour. Pouring sambuca into an espresso cup once the coffee is finished, which warms the spirit and adds a subtle coffee flavour, is another Italian tradition.

Sambuca formally emerged as a digestif during the 19th century and its reputation spread via *trattorie* restaurants throughout Italy. However, it is the Arabs who take the credit for introducing aniseed to Europe during their ninth-century occupation of Sicily. Zammu, which was a simple maceration of aniseed in water, was taken for its all-inclusive medicinal properties that supposedly cured absolutely everything from toothache to digestive problems. The Arabs also passed on their knowledge of distillation, and, by the Middle Ages, Sicilians were producing aniseed spirits.

Commercial production of aniseed drinks in France was started by Marie Brizard in 1755. As a charitable lady of Bordeaux, she attended patients in a local hospital where an African patient gave her the recipe for a traditional, restorative aniseed drink. It worked! Patients recovered, and charity became a business. The Marie Brizard company continues to produce a wide range of specialities.

Pernod was devised in Couvet, Switzerland, in 1792, although it was the work of a French doctor, Pierre Ordinaire, who had fled to Switzerland during the French Revolution. The mountains around Couvet were abundantly stocked with herbs, and as preparing medicinal elixirs from herbs was an essential part of his job, the doctor developed an infusion featuring star anise. Realizing the infusion was far more effective when steeped in alcohol, he concocted a liqueur called absinthe. This name was derived from the Latin for another key ingredient – wormwood (*Artemisia absinthum*), which had traditionally been prescribed for the treatment of gout and kidney stones. Nevertheless, a popular nickname for absinthe was *la Fée Verte* (the Green Fairy).

The entrepreneurial Major Henri Dubied acquired Ordinaire's recipe in 1797, and went into partnership with his son-in-law, Henri-Louis Pernod. Production was first based in Switzerland, then moved to Pontarlier, France, in 1805. Absinthe's enormous success resulted in it being sold under the Pernod brand name to distinguish it from the imitators that followed. These came to be known as pastiches – which is exactly what they were – and the word was subsequently abbreviated to pastis.

In the 1850s, Pernod was prescribed to soldiers to prevent malaria. Having acquired a taste for it, they drank Pernod off-duty as well. By the 1890s, it was the toast of Paris, having broadened its appeal to society darlings, intellectuals and bohemians. Degas, Picasso and Toulouse-Lautrec not only drank absinthe, but also painted Parisian scenes that revolved around it. Indeed, Toulouse-Lautrec never left home without absinthe, carrying a supply in a hollow walking stick. But the party had to end sometime, and at the beginning of the 20th century some sensational murder trials cited absinthe as the culprit, as it induced wild mood disorders, fits and hallucinations. Absinthe was on trial and the verdict was that a single ingredient – wormwood – was guilty. Its use was banned by the French government in 1915 and subsequently by various other European governments. Disastrous? Not at all; the production of aniseed spirits simply continued without it.

Although pastis and anise are often regarded as the same thing, it is a case of *vive la différence*. As an anise, Pernod focuses on aniseed, together with 14 other herbs ranging from camomile to veronica. A pastis such as Ricard uses aniseed and liquorice together with fennel, Provençal roots and other aromatic plants, resulting in a drier taste. Adding five parts water to one part anise or pastis, turning the liquid milky white, is the usual ratio and releases the full flavour. Ice is an optional extra. A deluxe pastis like Henri Bardouin is made with a total of 48 herbs and spices, and its intense flavour sees the recommended ratio of water to pastis increased to 6:1.

Absinthe continues to be produced in the Czech Republic, complete with wormwood, although the drink's alcoholic strength alone – 55 per cent abv, or higher – is capable of a significant effect. The traditional serving routine is to dip a teaspoon of caster sugar in a glass of absinthe. Once the sugar has absorbed some liquid, it is held just above the surface and ignited. As the sugar caramelizes, it is dripped into the

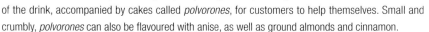

glass – which can also ignite the surface of the absinthe. Once all the sugar has been transferred, the absinthe is diluted with water, extinguishing any persistent flames in the process, and is ready to drink.

In Spain, anise is available in two styles – seco (dry) and dulce (sweet) – served mixed or on the rocks. While both are all-day drinks, seco is the more typical aperitif, with dulce usually a digestif and a partner for pastries and desserts. (Both are also available as chinchon, a separate type of anise named after a town 30 miles from Madrid, which has long been acclaimed for the quality of its production.) A typical way to drink anise in Spain is in a rustic double act called *sol y sombra* (sun and shade), with alternate sips of brandy. Anise is also popular with morning coffee and *churros* (breakfast fritters). A Christmas tradition sees Spanish shopkeepers putting out trays with glasses of the drink, accompanied by cakes called *polvorones*, for customers to help themselves. Small and crumbly, *polvorones* can also be flavoured with anise, as well as ground almonds and cinnamon.

Chatting over a glass of ouzo is an essential element of socializing in Greece. Based on grape spirit, ouzo is flavoured with aniseed and other aromatics such as fennel. It is typically drunk with ice, or mixed with one part water to two parts ouzo, which turns the liquid cloudy. Wherever there is ouzo, there are always mezze (hors d'oeuvres). Dropping into someone's house for an ouzo typically means a spread of olives, bread and cheese. Meanwhile, in a *kafenion* (coffee shop), where men play backgammon, ouzo is served with coffee throughout the day, with a simple selection of mezze such as olives or *toursi* (pickled vegetables). Ordering a carafe of ouzo in an ouzo bar yields a more extensive selection of mezze. The good news is that each time a carafe is ordered, it comes with a different set of mezze. A first round means light, simple dishes such as taramasalata, fried fish, fried aubergine or whole peppers. And as more ouzo is ordered, so the dishes and flavours become more involved.

In the Lebanon, a glass of arak – usually equal parts arak and water, on the rocks – is accompanied by the toast 'sahtak' ('your health'). Arak is produced from grape spirit and aniseed, and aficionados can enjoy deluxe styles such as Kasarak, which is aged for 18 months in earthenware jars. Starting the evening with arak tends to mean staying with it for the duration, with an accompaniment of classic mezze, such as *fattoush* (a salad with sumac and toasted pitta bread) or *tabbouleh*. Needless to say, arak is popular as a digestif too, with a light arak meaning one part arak to three parts water.

A selection of mezze also accompanies raki in Turkey. Popular since the 17th century, raki is produced from raisin or grape spirit, redistilled with aniseed. Raki comes in two strengths – 45 or 50 per cent abv, the latter offering a more intense aniseed experience – either accompanied by a glass of soda water or diluted with water, which turns it cloudy and accounts for its popular name of lion's milk. At the very least, accompanying mezze include honeydew melon, feta cheese and bread, while a more elaborate spread results in a *raki sofrasi* (raki table) featuring the likes of taramasalata, hummus, dolmas and imam bayildi, which translates, literally, as 'the priest fainted'. This combination of aubergine stuffed with onions and tomatoes was first served to a priest who allegedly passed out with gastronomic ecstasy. *Raki muhabbet* refers to the fine art of dining, drinking and conversation, with this originally all-male session increasingly an equal-opportunity event. The focus is on friendship, summed up by the saying, 'Cam cama degil, can cana' ('Not glass to glass, but soul to soul').

cp

10ml (2 tsp) lemon juice
20ml (4 tsp) anise or pastis
1 tsp caster sugar
2 ice cubes

Pour the lemon juice into a shaker, add the anise or pastis and sprinkle in the sugar. Shake well. Place the ice cubes in a tumbler, then strain the cocktail over the top.

iceberg

A few ice cubes
25ml (1½ tbsp) Pernod, or other premium anise
Dash of crème de menthe (mint liqueur)
125ml sparkling lemonade

Place the ice cubes in a Highball or tall glass, add the Pernod and crème de menthe, then pour in the lemonade.

flatline

20ml (4 tsp) sambuca or ouzo
A few drops of Tabasco
A squeeze of lemon juice or lime juice
20ml (4 tsp) blanco (white or silver) or reposado tequila

Pour the sambuca or ouzo into a shot glass, and add a drop or two of Tabasco. Squeeze some lemon or lime juice over the top, then pour in the tequila.

black martini

Ice cubes for mixing
50ml (3½ tbsp) vodka or gin, chilled
30ml (2 tbsp) black sambuca
Dash of Cointreau orange liqueur
Garnish: twist of orange

Place a few ice cubes in a mixing glass and pour in the vodka or gin, sambuca and a dash of Cointreau. Stir a few times to combine the ingredients, then strain into a Martini glass. Garnish with a twist of orange.

high flyer

A few ice cubes
25ml (1½ tbsp) Pernod, or other premium anise
75ml (5 tbsp) orange juice
75ml (5 tbsp) sparkling lemonade

Place the ice cubes in a Highball or tall glass and pour in the Pernod. Add the orange juice and finish off with the lemonade.

above left: *iceberg* **right:** *tomate* **far right:** *pastis riviera*

hand, with the assistance of a double-pronged tool, which is called a devil's fork. The roots are either macerated in spirit, or distilled, yielding two separate spirits that are subsequently blended and heightened by herb extracts. Nevertheless, gentian wasn't the starting point for Fernand Moureaux, the distillery owner who devised Suze during the 1880s. In fact, he had two criteria for his new aperitif: that it should be a spirit-based recipe, not wine-based, as was then the fashion in France, and also have a simple name. Rather than being the decision of a board-room think-tank, the short name may have been inspired by Moureaux's sister-in-law, Suzanne, fondly known as Suze, who was a great fan of gentian liqueurs.

Geography, rather than affinity, provided the name Angostura. This bitters was named after the Venezuelan town of Angostura, now called Cuidad Bolivar, where its creator, Dr Johann Siegert, was stationed. A German surgeon who

had enlisted in General Bolivar's liberation army, he finalized his formula for an aromatic bitters in 1824. Designed as preventative medicine for the military, particularly for warding off stomach ailments, it was the result of four years' experimentation with gentian, various tropical herbs and spices. The Royal Navy also prescribed Angostura as a prophylactic, but taken with gin to temper the distinctive flavour of the bitters. This yielded the Pink Gin (see page 37), a combination that extended beyond the Royal Navy to become a society favourite. Angostura's subsequent renown as a versatile ingredient is epitomized by the classic rum punch recipe of lime juice, sugar syrup, rum and Angostura.

The Italian taste for bitters is evident in various brands, some of which are purely regional favourites. However, Milan is home to two international blockbusters: Fernet Branca and Campari. Drawing on herbs from around the world, Fernet Branca dates from 1845. Served neat or with a dash of mineral water as a digestif, it is also added to espresso, to create a *caffe corretto*. Brancamenta is the mint version of the drink, with a blend of mint leaves, blossoms and aromatic herbs, providing a fresh, soothing sensation. Meanwhile, Campari's fabulous rich red colour makes it instantly recognizable as one of the world's classic aperitifs. Italians like to combine it with soda, ice and a slice of orange to make a Camparino. Adding a light, dry white wine provides a favourite Sunday lunch aperitif, while sparkling wine converts it into a Campari Spritzer.

The amazing combination of herbs, spices, dried fruit and barks was originally created by Gaspare Campari in 1862. Originally a liquoriste in Turin's most famous restaurant, Cambio, which was frequented by King Vittorio Emanuelle II, Campari then moved on to Milan where he established his own café-bar in the Galleria, one of Europe's most fashionable promenades. It was in the cellar of these premises that Gaspare Campari created his eponymous speciality. By the early 20th century, the next generation of Camparis was hosting the elite, with patrons such as King Edward VII of Great Britain and Ernest Hemingway. The company also gained a warrant to provide Campari for the Pope's table. Royalty, literati, glitterati, as well as religious leaders – Campari has charmed them all.

cardinale

A few ice cubes for mixing
Several drops Campari
45ml (3 tbsp) gin
10ml (2 tsp) dry vermouth
Garnish: strip of orange zest

Place a few ice cubes in a mixing
glass and pour in the Campari,
then mix in the gin and vermouth.
Strain into a cocktail glass and garnish
with a strip of orange zest.

champs elysées

Dash of Angostura bitters
25ml (1½ tbsp) Yellow Chartreuse liqueur
25ml (1½ tbsp) cognac
Juice of ½ lemon

Place a dash of Angostura bitters in
a cocktail glass, then add the Chartreuse
and cognac and pour on the lemon juice.

the charger

2–3 dashes of Angostura bitters
Club soda or sparkling mineral water,
    chilled, to top up
Garnish: slice of lemon and cocktail olive

Place some Angostura bitters in a
tall glass, then add the soda or mineral
water. Garnish with a slice of lemon
and a cocktail olive.

double vision

A few ice cubes
Dash of Angostura bitters
25ml (1½ tbsp) Absolut Citron,
    or other lemon vodka
25ml (1½ tbsp) Absolut Kurant,
    or other blackcurrant vodka
25ml (1½ tbsp) lime juice
100ml apple juice

Place the ice cubes in a Highball or tall
glass and add a dash of Angostura bitters.
Add the lemon and currant vodkas and the
lime juice, then pour in the apple juice.

hardtail

Ice cubes for shaker
15ml (1 tbsp) Jagermeister or
   Gammel Dansk bitters
15ml (1 tbsp) Cointreau or Grand Marnier
   orange liqueur
Dash of lime cordial or lime juice
Garnish: slice of lime

Into a shaker half-full with ice, pour the
bitters, Cointreau or Grand Marnier and
a dash of lime cordial or lime juice. Shake
then strain into a shot glass or tumbler.
Garnish with a slice of lime.
   Alternatively, place a few ice cubes
in a shot glass, pour in the bitters and the
Cointreau and add a dash of lime cordial or
lime juice. Garnish with a slice of lime.

highland fling

15ml (1 tbsp) orange bitters
25ml (1½ tbsp) blended Scotch whisky
25ml (1½ tbsp) blue curaçao
   orange liqueur
Soda water, chilled, to top up
Garnish: slices of kiwi fruit and starfruit

Pour the orange bitters into a tall glass,
then add the whisky and blue curaçao. Top
up with soda water and garnish with slices
of kiwi fruit and starfruit.

jager tonic

A few ice cubes
40ml (2½ tbsp) Jagermeister bitters
Tonic water, chilled, to top up
Garnish: slices of lemon and orange

Place a few ice cubes in a Highball or tall
glass, then pour in the Jagermeister and
top up with tonic water. Garnish with slices
of lemon and orange.

long hot summer

A handful of crushed ice
15ml (1 tbsp) Campari
Dash of Angostura bitters
50ml (3½ tbsp) blended Scotch whisky
Small chunks of cucumber, lemon
   and orange
Sprig of fresh mint
Lemonade, to top up

Place the crushed ice in a Highball or
tall glass and pour over the Campari,
Angostura bitters and whisky. Add a few
pieces of cucumber, lemon and orange
and sprinkle on some mint leaves, then
top up with lemonade.

montana

25ml (1½ tbsp) Campari
50ml (3½ tbsp) grapefruit juice
Dash of Lejay crème de cassis, or
   other premium blackcurrant liqueur

Pour the Campari into a Highball or tall
glass, then add the grapefruit juice. Add
a dash of crème de cassis.

trinidad cocktail

*Angostura bitters may only be used a few
dashes at a time, but as so many recipes
call for it, you'll soon need another bottle.*

4 dashes of Angostura bitters
50ml (3½ tbsp) Bacardi white rum,
   or other premium white rum
25ml (1½ tbsp) lime juice
1 tsp icing sugar
A small handful of crushed ice
Garnish: strip of lime zest

Drizzle the bitters into a shaker and add the
rum, lime juice and sugar, then shake. Place
the ice in a cocktail glass and pour over
the rum mixture. Garnish with the lime zest.

specialities

As taste becomes increasingly cosmopolitan, national specialities such as aquavit (akvavit), kummel, korn and schnapps can easily find themselves dismissed as anachronistic and parochial. But, with their unique heritage and nostalgic appeal, specialities will inevitably become fashionable again, however long they may have to wait in the wings. After all, every generation prides itself on rediscovering tradition.

The herbs and spices that helped endear aquavit to the Nordic palate were also behind its medicinal reputation. This is why Norwegians say: 'The greater the number of herbs and spices, the greater the number of diseases cured.' It's certainly more encouraging than another Norwegian aquavit-ism: 'The worse the taste, the better the results.' A more practical reason for adding flavourings such as caraway, juniper, angelica, anis and hypericum was to disguise aquavit's original robustness before the advent of rectification improved quality. This dates from 1846 when a Polish distiller, Isidor Henius, who had mastered the art of distilling potato vodka, set up in the Danish town of Aalborg. Trying his hand at akvavit (that's how it's spelled in Denmark), he produced Aalborg Taffel – still affectionately known as Red Aalborg after the red details on the label – which has a distinctive caraway flavour. Dill and coriander characterize the milder, golden-coloured Aalborg Jubilaeums, launched to celebrate Red Aalborg's 100th anniversary. While Danish akvavit is distilled from grain rather than potatoes, Norwegian aquavit continues to use potato spirit, flavoured with herbs and spices such as caraway, dill, aniseed, sweet fennel and coriander. It is matured in casks used to age oloroso sherry, which give the spirit its golden colour and hints of vanilla, while the residual sherry contributes a subtle sweetness.

Among the most celebrated Norwegian aquavits is Lysholm Linie, which was inadvertently created by Jorgen B Lysholm. In an attempt to develop his drinks business overseas, he dispatched some potato spirit to the East Indies in 1805, which entailed crossing the equator. But it didn't sell, and back it came. However, he discovered that the spirit had improved considerably en route. And that's how it's been aged ever since. Every month a new batch is sent on a four-and-a-half-month world cruise, crossing the equator twice, when it is refined by the constant, gentle rolling action and influence of the sea air.

Aquavit is served ice cold in small, long-stemmed glasses, and the drinking routine follows Nordic tradition. Everyone lifts their glass, makes eye contact, nods and says: 'Skal.' Heartier drinkers down it in one; others sip. Emptied glasses are also kept aloft, as everyone renews eye contact and nods again. Then it's time for another. The drinking circle in Denmark always includes hors d'oeuvres, such as salted herring fillets. In fact, herrings aren't served without akvavit, in line with the saying: 'You have to let the fish swim.' This makes akvavit essential at lunchtime with a smorgasbord, as well as traditional dishes such as *skipper lobescoves* (mashed potatoes with salt beef) and *gule aerter* (thick soup made from yellow split peas garnished with pork belly). Akvavit also accompanies fish courses at dinner, before re-appearing as a digestif with coffee. Norwegians, meanwhile, serve aquavit as an aperitif and digestif, but also enjoy it with food and between courses. Rich or salty dishes are accompanied and followed by aquavit. And the ultimate digestif, aged for ten years, is appropriately called Gilde Non Plus Ultra.

Caraway seeds provide the distinctive flavour behind kummel. Light chilling accentuates kummel's fresh, delicate flavour, which is usually served neat, as an aperitif or digestif. However, kummel does feature in a classic cocktail, Silver Bullet, combined with vodka (see page 99). Originating in either Germany, Denmark or the Netherlands, the production of kummel extended to France and Russia by the end of the 19th century. Nevertheless kummel's global headquarters was the Latvian capital of Riga.

Schnapps historically meant a 'swallow' or 'gulp' in German, although it is certainly worth lingering over, with a range of styles produced from grain or potatoes. Although Germans and Austrians traditionally drink schnapps neat, the former chill it while the latter generally don't, on the premise that it's easier to appreciate a premier example at room temperature. In fact, it tends to be poor quality schnapps that is chilled in Austria – an effective way to mask any faults. Strict quality control is undertaken by connoisseurs who dip a finger in the schnapps, rub it on the wrist, and evaluate the aroma. An Austrian phrase serves a similar purpose: 'If schnapps burns in the mouth, it's no good.'

Consumption is greatest in the Tyrol region, although schnapps is invariably served as a welcome drink anywhere in the Austrian countryside. This may be accompanied by a schnapps song, also a standard number at any rousing schnapps session, which includes the memorable line: 'Schnapps was his last word, then the angels took him away.' The most popular flavours in Austria are *obstler* (apple and pear), quince, mirabelle, plum and cherry. Flavoured styles also enjoy relationships with specific dishes. Cherry is often added to cheese fondue, *obstler* is a favourite digestif after pork or spare ribs, while dipping preserved plums in plum schnapps allows you to compare the fruit before and after distillation.

Korn is technically a type of schnapps, produced from a wide range of grains, but the terms korn and kornbrand can only be applied to spirits produced in German-speaking regions. The spirit's popularity rests on its digestif status, when it's drunk chilled, but not down in one; the correct way to appreciate korn is by allowing it to roll over the tongue. And if there's one thing better than korn, it's DoppelKorn, literally 'double pleasure', with a smooth but robust taste based on wheat.

A popular notion in the Netherlands is that everyone loves advocaat, but no one will admit it. Why not? This wonderful drink is even available in two styles. Thick advocaat is consumed using a small spoon, accompanied by a biscuit. The more liquid style is traditionally served with lemonade as a Snowball (see page 99), although drinking it on the rocks, and with mixers such as bitter lemon, is increasingly popular. 'Advocaat' is thought to be a corruption of the Portuguese-Brazilian word 'avocado'. Portuguese colonials used avocado pulp to prepare an alcoholic drink that was brought back to the Netherlands by Dutch settlers. Somehow the name stuck, even though egg yolks have replaced the avocado pulp and are combined with brandy, sugar and vanilla. The brand Warninks is synonymous with the drink, which means a very busy egg-breaking department that gets through around 18,000 eggs an hour.

An ancient tradition of fortifying and flavouring wine lies behind vermouth. While the original reasons for doing this were entirely practical, vermouth has long been considered a speciality. The Egyptians were among the first to fortify wine, principally to stabilize it during hot weather, while the Greeks and Romans added wormwood, thyme, rosemary and myrtle to revive wine that was losing flavour. At the royal court of Bavaria, during the 16th century, these distinctive wines acquired the name 'wermut' – German for wormwood, which was one of the key ingredients. A subsequent vogue at the French royal court saw 'wermut' become 'vermouth'.

Commercial production of vermouth originated in Turin during the 18th century. Among the early pioneers were two brothers, Carlo Stefano and Giovanno Giacomo Cinzano, with Casanova one of their more notorious customers. Giovanno's grandson, Francesco Cinzano, opened a vermouth shop on Turin's fashionable Via Dora Grossa in 1816. Locals called this the Road to Fortune, as it housed all the most successful shops. They were right, and Cinzano went on to became an international success. Fellow Piedmont phenomenon Martini & Rossi dates from 1847. After years of experimentation, chief herbalist and wine-maker Luigi Rossi devised a recipe for the famous vermouth, drawing on more than a dozen ingredients, including sandalwood, roses and marjoram.

Two indigenous grape varieties of l'Hérault in south-west France, picpoul and clairette, form the basis of Noilly Prat. Wines from both varieties are aged in separate cellars for a year, before another bout of ageing – al fresco. Three years later, they are blended with French spirits and 20 herbs. The elegant result combines herbaceousness with depth of flavour. It is also excellent for cooking.

Unfortunately, it's a tough time for vermouth sales. But however much the international market may slide, vermouth will always enjoy a sublime liaison with vodka or gin in the Dry Martini (see page 110). This may only be a supporting role – a few drops at most – but so what? The Dry Martini is, and always will be, the world's ultimate cocktail.

apfel cha cha

25ml (1½ tbsp) Berentzen Apfelkorn,
   or other premium apple schnapps
50ml (3½ tbsp) coconut cream
25ml (1½ tbsp) pineapple juice
15ml (1 tbsp) single cream
Garnish: slice of apple and wedge of lime

Pour the apple schnapps, coconut cream,
pineapple juice and cream into a shaker
and shake. Pour the mixture into a cocktail
glass and garnish it with a slice of apple
and a wedge of lime.

absolut angel

Ice cubes for shaker
25ml (1½ tbsp) apple schnapps
50ml (3½ tbsp) Absolut vodka, or other
   premium grain vodka
10ml (½ tbsp) white crème de cacao
   (chocolate liqueur)
50ml (3½ tbsp) double cream
Garnish: freshly grated nutmeg

Into a shaker half-full with ice, pour the
apple schnapps and the vodka, then add
the chocolate liqueur and double cream
and shake. Strain into a Martini glass and
sprinkle with a dash of grated nutmeg.

aquatini

A few ice cubes for mixing
25–50ml (1½–3½ tbsp) Linie aquavit,
   or other premium aquavit
Dash of Noilly Prat, or other premium
   dry vermouth

Place a few ice cubes in a mixing glass,
pour in the aquavit and add a dash of
vermouth. Stir briefly then strain into a
Martini glass.

dorchester golden fizz

Ice cubes for shaking, plus a few ice cubes
25ml (1½ tbsp) peach schnapps
50ml (3½ tbsp) white rum
1 tsp sugar syrup
20ml (1½ tbsp) lemon juice
Dash of egg white
Lemonade, to top up

Into a shaker half-full with ice cubes, pour
the peach schnapps, white rum, sugar
syrup and lemon juice, then add a dash
of egg white. Shake well to froth up the
white. Place a few ice cubes in a Highball
or tall glass and strain in the rum mixture,
then top up with lemonade.

mountain creek

*Typically taken neat or with a side order
of herrings, aquavit also provides a base
for a variety of mixed drinks.*

A few ice cubes for mixing
25ml (1½ tbsp) Linie aquavit, or other
   premium aquavit
25ml (1½ tbsp) Vikingfjord vodka,
   or other premium grain vodka
Dash of lime juice
Sparkling lemonade, to top up

Place a few ice cubes in a tall glass, then
add the aquavit and vodka and a dash of
lime juice. Top up with lemonade.

specialities

*As we are naturally more experimental with
cocktails, it's an ideal opportunity for a first
taste of an unfamiliar speciality spirit.*

Sake is always accompanied by food, with a formal meal seeing a succession of dishes starting with raw fish, followed by boiled or steamed specialities, then a fried or grilled dish. When rice appears on the table, usually with the main course, it is the traditional sign to stop serving sake. This accounts for the distinct male trait of eating rice as late as possible during the meal, or avoiding it altogether.

The Japanese also use rice to produce shochu, a spirit that can equally be distilled from molasses, potatoes, sweet potatoes or various other grains. Now more socially acceptable, particularly owing to its popularity with the younger, stylish set, shochu was traditionally viewed as the preserve of the underclass. But even that was a step up from the status it held during the Edo period, from the 17th to the 19th century, when it was used as a disinfectant. Traditionally drunk neat – sometimes in a wooden container with a measure of salt on the side, like cold sake – shochu is also a typical accompaniment to sushi.

A recent trend is to serve shochu as a long drink. Adding soda water and a flavoured syrup, as well as ice and lemon, is one favourite. Another is ume shochu, with ume referring to *umeboshi*. Sometimes described as a plum, an *umeboshi* is technically an apricot, picked when unripe, then salted and weighed down to force out the liquid. Subsequently dried in the summer sun, *umeboshi* are also pickled with *shiso* leaves, which gives them a red hue. They are often served as an appetizer, when the salty-sour flavour is a real winner. *Umeboshi* are also an essential element of a traditional Japanese breakfast, together with grilled salmon or cod, rice, miso soup, seaweed and green tea. During the cocktail hour, an *umeboshi* and a measure of shochu, usually around one-fifth of the cup, are topped up with boiling water. While this combination is commonplace in bars and informal family gatherings, it's not yet considered quite smart enough to appear at cocktail parties.

Rice wine, together with various rituals, is essential during the traditional Chinese New Year celebrations. Practicalities come first, which means cleaning the house in the morning to ensure everything is ready for midnight; this also makes a symbolic 'clean start' for the New Year. Moreover, a feng shui master is frequently brought to the home, prior to New Year's Eve, to make any necessary adjustments to the living space. The afternoon is devoted to preparing dinner, but before the family eats, there are other considerations. New Year's Eve is when the kitchen god comes down to earth to see what has been happening in the household and report back to the Jade Emperor. Offerings to the god – usually rice wine and sweet pastries – are placed in the kitchen. Food may also be set out in the living room for the spirits of deceased relatives, who are believed to return to earth at this time.

Michiew (warmed rice wine) is served with the New Year's Eve dinner, which typically includes fish and various dumplings. Originally produced as a means of using up surplus stock, rice wine tends to be more popular in southern China. However, many devotees say the best quality rice wine is from the north, where it's produced in limited quantities. New Year's Day in China is devoted to the family, with 2 January seeing a continuation of the celebrations. This usually means visiting friends – with some rice wine or liqueurs in tow. Three days to celebrate the New Year? Now that's what I call a party, and as the Japanese poet Manyoshu wrote in the eighth century: 'Sitting silent and looking wise cannot be compared to drinking wine and making a racket.'

decibel

75ml (5 tbsp) overproof sake (40 abv),
  or Ketel One vodka or other premium
  neutral vodka, chilled
A few fresh lychees, peeled and pressed
  with the back of a spoon to extract
  25ml (1½ tbsp) juice

Chill a Martini glass. Pour the sake into
a mixing glass and add the lychee juice.
Stir and strain into the chilled glass.

fj

50ml (3½ tbsp) strong green tea, chilled
  (or use jasmine or hibiscus tea)
35ml (2½ tbsp) sake, chilled
Dash of premium dry vermouth

Pour the chilled tea into a mixing
glass, then add the sake and a dash
of vermouth. Stir and strain into a
Martini glass.

mei-fuwa

Ice cubes for shaker
50ml (3½ tbsp) sake or ume shu (plum wine)
25ml (1½ tbsp) Campari
60ml (4 tbsp) grapefruit juice

Into a shaker half-full with ice, pour
the sake or plum wine, Campari and
grapefruit juice. Shake and strain into
a Highball or tall glass.

hakusan haiku

*The less-is-more school of Japanese
haiku poetry is reflected in this minimalist
combination that yields a maximum effect.*

Ice cubes for mixing
50ml (3½ tbsp) Hakusan sake, or other
  premium sake
Dash of dry vermouth
Garnish: small pickled onion

Place a few ice cubes in a mixing glass,
add the sake and a dash of dry vermouth
and stir. Strain into a Martini glass and
garnish with a small pickled onion.

nobu blackcurrant sake

(Makes 1.5–2 litres)
500g fresh blackcurrants
Vanilla pod, split
1.5 litre still mineral water
250g caster sugar
500ml sake

Place the blackcurrants on a clean muslin
cloth, scrape the vanilla seeds over them
and drop in the pod. Tie the muslin into a
bag or pouch.

Pour the water into a large saucepan and
add the sugar, then pop in the muslin bag
and bring to the boil. Skim the surface to
remove any impurities. Reduce the heat
to low and leave to simmer for 1–1½ hours,
skimming the surface occasionally.

Leave the blackcurrant syrup to cool
then remove the muslin bag and place it in
an airtight container. Refrigerate the syrup
and the bag for up to 3 days.

Squeeze the muslin bag to extract as
much flavour as possible and discard it,
then strain the syrup through a fine sieve.
Pour in the sake and stir, then refrigerate
until cold. Serve in shot glasses or small
tumblers. Consume within 3 days.

top left: *mei-fuwa* right: *sake martini*

sake 1

25ml (5 tsp) sake
25ml (5 tsp) puréed raspberries
Dash of crème de framboise
    (raspberry liqueur)
Champagne, chilled, to top up
Garnish: fresh raspberry

Pour the sake into a champagne flute and add the raspberry purée and liqueur. Top up with champagne and stir gently, then add a fresh raspberry.

sake martini

A few ice cubes for mixing
25ml (1½ tbsp) sake
75ml (5 tbsp) Ketel One vodka or other
    premium grain neutral vodka
Dash of Lillet, or a premium dry vermouth
Dash of orange bitters
Garnish: paper-thin slices of cucumber

Place a few ice cubes in a mixing glass and pour on the sake, then add the vodka. Add a dash each of Lillet and orange bitters and stir, then strain the drink into a Martini glass. To serve, lay cucumber slices across the top of the glass so that the drink flows through them.

cocktails

As one of the world's most international words, 'cocktail' is not translated or substituted in any language. It's the Esperanto of the bar set because, wherever you are, you can at least be sure of ordering a cocktail.

Various countries have a tradition of serving mixed drinks, which makes it much harder to trace the origin of 'cocktail'. One theory involves an 18th-century Mexican princess, Coctel, whose father, Axolotl XVIII, was negotiating a border treaty with an American general. Once an agreement had been reached, Coctel offered up a gold, bejewelled cup containing a mixed drink with which to seal the deal. But who should take the first sip, and without causing offence? Coctel solved the problem by ceremoniously drinking the contents herself. The general declared that the princess's name, which when pronounced American-style was, more or less, 'cocktail', would always be honoured by the American army.

Some other theories seem credible; others don't. English taverns used to serve a drink comprising various spirits with which to toast the winner of a cock fight – the victor being the cock left with the most tail feathers at the end, or, indeed, left alive. The tail feather of a cock may also have been used to stir or garnish such

a drink. Then again, French soldiers joining up with George Washington's army during the American War of Independence took a favourite mixed drink with them: a wine-based speciality of Bordeaux called coquetel.

The earliest record of 'cocktail' appearing in print was in the American periodical *The Balance* in 1806: 'Cocktail is a stimulating liquor, composed of spirits of any kind, sugar, water and bitters.' That definition was at least a start, with the first book of cocktail recipes published in 1862. *How to Mix Drinks, or the Bon Vivant's Companion* was written by a renowned New York bartender called 'Professor' Jerry Thomas. Bartender and entrepreneur Harry Johnson was behind another landmark tome, *The Bartender's Manual, or How to Mix Drinks of the Present Style*, published in 1882.

The 1920s and '30s were the golden age of cocktails, in spite of Prohibition which made the production, sale and distribution of alcohol illegal. Ironically, bootlegging and speakeasies flourished, resulting in the prison population doubling in the first four years of Prohibition. Numerous cocktails were created, partly through necessity. Bootleg spirit, known as moonshine, was of variable quality, and skilful mixing was often required to make it drinkable, let alone enjoyable. The Screwdriver is a prime example; the crude flavour of vodka was disguised by adding orange juice, but orange juice at the time was canned and didn't taste good either, so sugar was added to compensate.

As cocktails are also about fashion, whether a new creation becomes a fashion victim or exceeds its happy hour to become a classic is impossible to predict. Every decade has seen a cocktail revival, marked by its own specific characteristics. The 1980s design brief was kitsch exuberance: too many flavours crammed into each recipe, and too many accessories crammed into each glass. Umbrellas, sparklers, plastic animals and stirrers were crowned by that icon of the *déclassé* – the glacé cherry. The millennium cocktail agenda, on the other hand, is a streamlined reinterpretation with simpler, more sophisticated flavour combinations and presentations. This has inevitably revived the Dry Martini (see page 110) which has a mystique and status that other classic cocktails can only dream about.

While the Dry Martini merely combines gin or vodka with dry vermouth, the ingredients transcend their individual merits to yield a truly sublime result. Needless to say, various 'movers and shakers' claim to have invented the Dry Martini. Perhaps it was Julio Richelieu, a bartender in Martinez, California, who was asked by a prospector in the 1870s to make the finest cocktail money could buy; the gold nuggets he placed on the bar were undoubtedly an incentive. The result was a Martinez Special with gin, vermouth and a dash of orange bitters. A name change later, it's an early Martini. Maybe. Martini di Arma di Taggia also staked his claim. A bartender at the Knickerbocker Hotel, New York, he began serving Martinis – equal parts gin, dry vermouth and a dash of orange bitters – around 1910. This may have been an original recipe, or an adaptation, as similar combinations were already veterans of the cocktail circuit. Incidentally, orange bitters remained a feature of the Dry Martini until the 1950s.

Preparing a Dry Martini may appear simple, but this cocktail is considered the supreme test of a barman's ability, as every stage entails decisions that have a profound influence on the end result. The first decision is: gin or vodka? Purists insist on gin, and use the terms Vodka Martini or Vodkatini to establish the vital difference. Specifying the gin or vodka is also important, as distinctions between brands tasted neat will remain apparent when Martini-fied. The Dry Martini has been getting drier ever since it was first established, with the original ratio of equal parts vermouth and gin now down to a few drops of vermouth. Nevertheless, those few drops are significant enough to raise the question: which vermouth? Noilly Prat is the traditionalists' choice, on the premise that it was used in the 'original' version from the Knickerbocker Hotel. Noilly Prat's appeal also rests on its rich, herbaceous flavour, but this is too over-powering for other Martini-ites who opt for the subtler, drier Martini & Rossi Extra Dry.

How to combine the ingredients is a crucial consideration. While shaking was used originally, stirring has long been established as the norm. Shaking is largely condemned on the basis that the ice over-dilutes the cocktail, particularly if a barman is prone to extended shaking. While this action may look impressive, the cocktail is as cold as it can get within about ten seconds. Any longer and it's merely a case of adding more water from melting ice. Stirring over ice also entails some dilution, but less than shaking, and this is often considered an asset as the cocktail is not composed entirely of alcohol. A popular guideline is to stir 12 times with a metal spoon, carefully, to avoid cracking the ice which could result in a cocktail with tiny ice flakes. As vermouth goes into the mixing glass first, another option is to stir the vermouth over ice and drain the liquid, so the ice cubes are merely coated with vermouth. One way to avoid the shake or stir debate is to build, by pouring a few drops of vermouth into a Martini glass, and then pouring over the gin or vodka – technically a Diamond Martini (see page 110).

Whatever the style of Martini, the experience will be sensational only if it is served really cold. And as a Dry Martini is invariably drunk slowly, maintaining the correct temperature for the duration is a real challenge. To avoid relying on ice for the entire chill factor means keeping the gin or vodka, as well as the glasses, in the freezer. Subsequently, as the temperature rises slightly, the spirit opens up to reveal its characteristics, which is an intriguing added extra.

Choosing between an olive or a twist is another major commitment. A twist adds the refreshing nature of lemon zest – from unwaxed specimens, and excluding the bitter pith – which is a counter-point to vodka and a complement to gin's citrus flavours. The influence of the lemon can be subtle, restricted to a thread of zest floating on the surface, or more dominant, achieved by wiping the rim of the glass with a lemon wedge and releasing the essential oils by twisting the zest. An olive adds a mellow, savoury tone, and since it also absorbs some of the cocktail, eating it provides an ideal conclusion to the Dry Martini experience. To intensify the flavour, a little olive brine can be added, and as this lends the cocktail a cloudy appearance it is called a Dirty Martini. Substituting a black olive for the usual green results in a Buckeye Martini, with flavoured olives such as almond, jalapeño pepper, garlic or anchovy extending the choice. Adding a pearl onion instead of an olive or a twist turns a Dry Martini into a Gibson.

The latest development of the Dry Martini is the Flavoured Martini; in fact, Martini is increasingly used as a generic term for flavoured vodka cocktails prepared using the Dry Martini principle, and served in a Martini glass. Flavoured Martinis can include vodka infused with ginger to yield a Ginger Martini, or mixed with a chocolate liqueur and orange bitters to give a Chocolate Martini. The Fresh Fruit Martini – ripe fruit such as pineapple or blackcurrants added to the shaker with a dash of the relevant fruit liqueur – is another player. 'But it's not a Martini,' cry the traditionalists and, of course, it isn't. It's a Flavoured Martini. We know the rules and respect them, because that's what makes a Dry Martini so perfect, but we also enjoy breaking the rules to see what comes out of the shaker next.

dry martini

Ice cubes for mixing

75ml (5 tbsp) gin or vodka

10ml (½ tbsp) dry vermouth

Garnish: strip of lemon zest or a green olive

Place a few ice cubes in a mixing glass, add the gin or vodka and the dry vermouth and stir. Strain into a Martini glass and garnish with lemon zest or an olive.

diamond martini

The level of vodka in this martini makes it an ultimate, but it won't work unless the glass and vodka are frozen.

Dash of Martini & Rossi Extra Dry
   vermouth, or other premium
   dry vermouth

125ml Wyborowa vodka, or other
   premium grain vodka, frozen

Wedge of lemon

Chill a Martini glass. Add the vermouth and vodka. Twist the lemon over the drink, then run the wedge around the rim of the glass.

perfect martini

70ml (4½ tbsp) Tanqueray gin, or other
   premium overproof gin, frozen

15ml (1 tbsp) dry vermouth

15ml (1 tbsp) sweet vermouth

Garnish: twist of lemon

Chill a Martini glass. Pour in the gin and vermouths and stir, then garnish with a twist of lemon.

nutty martini

Ice cubes for shaker
75ml (5 tbsp) vodka
20ml (1½ tbsp) Frangelico hazelnut liqueur
1 tsp sugar syrup

Into a shaker half-full with ice, pour the vodka and Frangelico and add the sugar syrup. Shake briefly, then strain into a Martini glass.

orange martini

Ice cubes for mixing
100ml orange vodka
Dash of Angostura bitters
Dash of orange juice
Dash of Cointreau orange liqueur
Dash of Grand Marnier orange liqueur

Place a few ice cubes in a mixing glass and add the vodka. Splash on some Angostura bitters, orange juice and some Cointreau and Grand Marnier and stir. Strain into a Martini glass.

sapphire martini

2 dashes of dry vermouth
2 dashes of blue curaçao orange liqueur
60ml (4 tbsp) Bombay Sapphire gin,
   or other premium gin, frozen
Garnish: twist of lemon

Chill a Martini glass. Add a couple of dashes each of dry vermouth and blue curaçao, then pour in the gin. Garnish with a twist of lemon.

cocktails

Every cocktail aspires to the status of the Dry Martini. It's the ultimate in sophistication, and preparing one is the ultimate test for any host.

left: *dry martini* **above right:** *sapphire martini*

pineapple martini

Slice of ripe pineapple, plus extra
    wedges of pineapple to garnish
50ml (3½ tbsp) vodka
Dash of sugar syrup
2–3 dashes of orange bitters
Ice cubes for shaker

Put the pineapple into a mixing glass and
add the vodka, sugar syrup and bitters.
Break down the fruit with a muddler or the
back of a spoon. Half-fill a shaker with ice
cubes, then add the fruit and vodka mix
and shake. Strain into a Martini or similar
cocktail glass, garnished with pineapple.

chocolate & orange martini

Chocolate, for glass rim
Ice cubes for shaker
35ml (2½ tbsp) Absolut vodka,
    or other premium grain vodka
15ml (1 tbsp) white crème de cacao
    (chocolate liqueur)
Dash of Cointreau or Grand Marnier
    orange liqueur

To make the chocolate rim, put chunks
of chocolate into a bowl and melt them
over a pan of simmering water. Pour
the melted chocolate onto a plate and dip
the rim of a Martini glass into it, then stand
the glass upright. Allow the chocolate rim
to set then chill the glass.

Into a shaker half-full with ice, pour
the vodka and crème de cacao and add a
dash of Cointreau or Grand Marnier. Shake
briefly then strain into the prepared glass.

polish martini

Ice cubes for shaker
25ml (5 tsp) Krupnik honey vodka,
    or other premium honey vodka
25ml (5 tsp) Wyborowa vodka,
    or other premium grain vodka
25ml (5 tsp) apple juice

Chill a Martini glass. Half-fill a shaker with
ice, then add the vodkas and apple juice
and shake briefly. Strain into the glass.

right: fruits of the forest martini **far right:** *pineapple martini*

fruits of the forest martini

2 each of fresh blackberries, blueberries,
   raspberries and strawberries, plus
   extra for garnish
2 dashes of orange bitters
50ml (3½ tbsp) Wyborowa lemon vodka,
   or 25ml (5 tsp) each of Wyborowa lemon
   and Soplica Polish vodka, or other
   premium grain vodkas
Ice cubes for shaker

Place the fruits in a mixing glass and
add some orange bitters and the vodka.
Break down the fruit with a muddler
or the back of a spoon.
   Half-fill a shaker with ice cubes,
pour in the fruit and vodka mix and
shake briefly. Strain the drink into
a Martini or similar cocktail glass and
garnish with the extra berries.

punches

The supreme versatility of punches and cups, offering any permutation of wines, spirits and non-alcoholic extras, and garnished with a potpourri of herbs and fruits, inevitably makes them vulnerable to abuse from the 'anything goes' school of party hosts. Cheap red wine? Open the box. Dodgy fruit? Chop it up and throw it in. Who will know once it's floating around in a punch bowl? And as for the flavour? Who cares, as long as there are plenty of ingredients.

Stop right there! Punch was never meant to degenerate into such a travesty of its role model. First prepared in India by English colonials at the beginning of the 17th century, punch was originally derived from the Hindu word *panch*, meaning 'five'. This referred to the number of ingredients used, which were sugar, lime juice, spices, water and alcohol in the form of arrack, prepared from fermented coconut water, rice and palm syrup.

It didn't take long for punch to become one of the first Indian take-aways. The English East India Company, formed in 1600, soon exported the recipe, and the ingredients, back home. Growing steadily in popularity, punch was circulating in the most fashionable English circles during the 18th century, when rum became

a popular stand-in for arrack. As punch was drunk hot, it meant a brief flambé prior to serving. Everyone loved this visual spectacle, and blowing out the flames was considered enormous fun. But the spectacle also had a practical purpose: to integrate the ingredients.

From its new English base, punch was soon flowing across Europe and Scandinavia. It became very popular in Sweden, also during the 18th century, where it was known as *dhen Angelska poins* (the English punch). The Swedish version typically combined arrack with sugar and lemon, with the East India Company supplying special cups for serving, as well as continued supplies of arrack. From the mid-19th century, the drink also captivated French palates, when everything *anglais* was *à la mode*. French recipes made use of colonial ingredients such as rum, as well as their national specialities like the sublime dessert wine sauternes. As a Marquise punch entails adulterating sauternes with sugar, lemons, cloves and cognac, not to mention raising the temperature, it's totally *de trop* for the sauternes set. A champagne punch dishes out a similar treatment, combining champagne with brandy, Cointreau, maraschino cherry liqueur and a final squirt of soda.

The Portuguese use their national speciality, port wine, to fortify a punch known as ponche, popularly called a fruit salad punch, due to an abundance of oranges, melons, bananas, mangoes and the like, together with moscatel wine. Similarly, a traditional style of genever known as brandewyn – literally 'burnt wine' – provides a punch at Dutch weddings. There are two versions, served according to gender. The vital difference is that boerenjongens (farmer boys) has raisins in the glass, while boerenmeisjes (farmer girls) has apricots. Once the punch has been drunk, the fruit is eaten with a spoon.

The summer season in Germany features specialities such as bowle. This combines sekt – German sparkling wine – with sweet or semi-sweet wine such as müller-thurgau, and sometimes soda water, as well as fresh fruit like strawberries and berries. Summer wine festivals throughout Germany are the perfect venues for enjoying variations on the bowle theme.

Summer parties in Finland revolve around different versions of booli, a vodka and white wine combination, extended with soft drinks like lemonade, and fruit, including apples, oranges, pineapples and bananas. Glogi takes over in Finland during the Christmas party season, which begins in mid-November. This hot mix of vodka and red or white wine, cinnamon and sugar, which is similar to Swedish glogg (see page 119), is served in cups and garnished with raisins and flaked almonds.

In Poland, vodka punch called krupnik, flavoured with honey, cinnamon, cloves and ginger, is the toast of Carnival, the traditional party season which lasts from Twelfth Night (5 January) until the eve of Lent on Shrove Tuesday. Carnival is also prime time for serving *paczki* (doughnuts filled with rose petal jam or plum preserve). On Shrove Tuesday, the traditional accompaniment to krupnik is *faworki*, literally 'little favours', also known as *chrusty* (brushwood) which gives a better idea of their appearance: delicate, deep-fried pastry twists dredged in icing sugar.

While rum punch is one of the most familiar punches, this term does not automatically mean a long drink. In fact, a rum punch in the French West Indies is a short drink, typically comprising a shot of white rum and sugar cane syrup, maybe with a few drops of lime juice, and garnished with lime zest. Throughout the rest of the Caribbean, rum punch is served in the usual way: length with strength. The origins of the drink are entirely practical: a simple way of making early robust forms of rum more palatable. The proportions were one part lime juice, two of sugar syrup, three parts rum, and four of water or milk. Although one short of the Indian formula, it hasn't stopped rum punch from becoming an

planter's punch

This punch was originally enjoyed by the planters who ran sugar plantations throughout the Caribbean.

Ice cubes for shaker, plus extra to serve
50ml (3½ tbsp) dark rum
25ml (1½ tbsp) lime juice
50ml (3½ tbsp) lemon juice
2 tsp caster sugar
Dash of orange bitters
Dash of Angosturas bitters
Soda water, to top up
Garnish: cocktail cherries, slices of
    lemon, lime and orange, and chunks
    of pineapple

Into a shaker half-full with ice, pour the rum, lime and lemon juice and sprinkle over the sugar. Add a dash each of orange and Angostura bitters and shake. Place a few ice cubes in a tall glass and strain the punch over them, then top up with soda water. Garnish with fruit.

sangria

(Makes about 5 litres)
Plenty of ice
2 litres sparkling lemonade
3–4 750ml bottles of red wine
100ml gin
100ml vodka
Caster sugar, to taste
2 each of oranges, bananas and apples,
    peeled and sliced
1 cinnamon stick

Place plenty of ice in a very large bowl, then pour in the lemonade, red wine, gin and vodka. Sprinkle in the sugar to taste, stir, then add the fruit and cinnamon and stir again. Taste and sprinkle in a little more sugar if required, stirring well to dissolve it before tasting and adding more. Serve in tall glasses.

hot drinks

Some people like to heat them, or even ignite them, while others avoid them altogether because when alcohol is served hot, it is usually dominated by the unmistakable flavours of cinnamon, ginger, nutmeg and cloves – the four classic hot drinks accessories.

Cinnamon's warm, subtly sweet taste derives from the inner bark of the Sri Lankan cinnamon tree, while ginger's pungent flavour stems from the aromatic root of a plant native to Southeast Asia. Indonesia is the original source of nutmeg – the distinctive seed of the nutmeg tree – as well as cloves, with their rich, penetrating flavour. These dried, unopened flower buds resembling drawing pins are incredibly user-friendly, and can be stuck straight into orange or lemon zest – two essential accoutrements for preparing hot drinks.

A prime beneficiary of these flavourings is grzane piwo, literally 'heated beer' – a staple in Poland and eastern Europe. It can be a simple matter of heating beer with sugar or lemon zest, and adding spices such as cloves and cinnamon. Another favourite pairing is honey and nutmeg, together with egg yolks for an enriching effect. Porterowka is also a hot favourite at Polish parties, but in this case it's not the spices that provide the kick – equal parts of stout and porter beer are reinforced by the same amount of Polish Rectified Spirit. Not only is this the strongest spirit in Poland but, at a whopping 95 per cent abv, it enjoys the same elevated status around the world. Warmed vodka is also the base for instant flavourings in Poland, where it is poured over honey and cloves, fresh mint leaves or freshly ground peppercorns.

Schnapps (see page 94) is the key to jagertea, heated together with red wine and spices, which is a popular way to round off a day's skiing in Switzerland. An equivalent in Germany and Austria is glüh-wein, a version of mulled wine, which is prepared by heating red wine sweetened with sugar, and flavouring it with lemon or orange zest and the usual cast of spices – cinnamon, cloves, and so on. Some skiers stop at huts half-way down a run and drink glühwein even before it's all over.

As an essential element of the Swedish Christmas season, and specifically Christmas Eve, glogg can be either an aperitif, or the welcome drink at a party (see page 119 for a glogg Christmas punch). There are three principal styles flavoured with spices: non-alcoholic, a red wine base, and wine combined with spirits such as vodka. Less traditional but increasingly popular is white glogg, using white wine. Glogg is usually prepared a couple of days prior to serving, to allow the flavours to fuse. Needless to say, in this age of convenience products, each style of glogg is available as a pre-mix, as are bottles of spiced concentrate for adding to the wines of your choice. Glogg is traditionally served in small glasses or espresso-sized china cups, with guests placing almonds and raisins in their cup before ladling it on top.

Although usually taken neat as a digestif, port can also be combined with boiling water, sugar and the likes of cinnamon, cloves and nutmeg to create a Negus, a British favourite. Scotch whisky, mean-while, is the basis for the medicinal, rather than the sociable, hot toddy – mixed with hot water, honey and lemon. De luxe versions add cinnamon and cloves. Irish whiskey is just as easy to convert into the traditional Hot Irish (see page 127), served in every Irish pub, by adding brown sugar, a pinch of cinnamon and half a lemon slice studded with cloves, topped up with hot water.

'Tom and Jerry' is an American term for a gregarious young man about town, and is subsequently the evocative name for a drink. Recipes vary from a straightforward combination of rum and spices to more elaborate versions such as a base of warmed bourbon, rum, a dash of brandy and hot milk into which beaten egg yolks and brown sugar are added, followed by a topping of egg whites beaten with white sugar, and sprinkled with cinnamon. America's early settlers also enjoyed hot rum drinks, with rum one of the first spirits distilled in New England, using molasses imported from the Caribbean. The Flip was typical, made with rum and mulled by using a red hot poker known as a loggerhead.

Grog – rum, boiling water, honey or sugar and lemon juice – was originally a Royal Navy drink. It stemmed from Admiral Edward Vernon's decree in 1740 that the sailors' rum ration be diluted with water (see also page 48). A richer option is hot buttered rum (see page 127). The name almost says it all: a knob of butter melts on the surface of a rum-and-boiling-water combination, which is flavoured with spices such as cinnamon, nutmeg and vanilla. Rum is also a traditional way of fortify-ing hot (or iced) tea. As well as providing the length in long drinks, tea serves a useful role by balancing the sweetness of the alcohol, while the tannins give body.

The European love for hot chocolate began as early as the 16th century when the Spanish conquis-tadores in Mexico dispatched cocoa beans back home to Spain. The Spanish knew exactly how to get the best out of the beans, which the Aztecs prepared with honey and vanilla. Because of its initial

rarity, hot chocolate became the hallmark of the most fashionable salons of Europe, but by the 18th century, it had become more commonplace and was even dispensed by street vendors. The French now enjoy adding Green Chartreuse to their hot chocolate during the winter, while the Danes take it with a glass of Grand Marnier on the side.

While tea and chocolate enjoy brief liaisons with alcohol, coffee is a far more committed partner. Credit for discovering its enlivening properties goes to a medieval Abyssinian goatherd named Kaldi, who noticed that his flock became frisky after nibbling the berries of a certain bush. After eating the berries himself, he became just as playful, and spread the word. Soon the berries were eaten to help the devout keep awake during all-night prayer vigils. Boiling water poured over the berries produced a palatable drink, but when some berries accidentally fell into a fire and released their wonderful aroma, it became customary to roast them first. In religious as well as secular communities, coffee became established as a social drink among Arabs during the 15th century, reaching Europeans by the 17th century.

Coffee alongside a glass of something stronger is popular in various countries. In Iceland, it's usually accompanied by Grand Marnier, while rum is preferred in northern Germany, and kirsch in Switzerland. Latvians, meanwhile, turn to their national drink – Black Balsam. Italians may drink grappa alongside espresso, or after the espresso by pouring it into the empty cup to pick up a little coffee flavour. Another Italian practice during the summer is to drink coffee from a cup wiped around the rim with a wedge of lemon, with a glass of iced Limoncello on the side.

Alcohol added to coffee is popular at any time of the day – starting with breakfast. Older, and wiser, Italians typically have a slug of grappa in their morning espresso, which is known as *caffe corretto*; *corretto* merely indicates the presence of alcohol. Similarly, *café-calva* sees a shot of calvados providing a kick-start to the day in Normandy, while manual workers in Spain take a *carajillo* (coffee with anise) in the morning, with practically everyone else having one after lunch. Other alcoholic coffees enjoyed later in the day are *café Barcelona*, made with Spanish brandy and whipped cream, while Flemish coffee contains a shot of genever. The Swiss enjoy kirsch in *Kaffee fertig*, which, literally, means finished or ready, whereas *Kaffee lutz* is schnapps with black coffee served in a goblet. In Austria, it's typically cherry or pear schnapps that flows into coffee, which is then topped with whipped cream.

Cremat is another Spanish favourite, combining coffee with brandy, rum, cinnamon and lemon zest, which is briefly flamed to integrate the flavours. In the region of Cognac, flames also feature in the traditional *brûlot charentais*. Cognac is poured in a saucer on which a cup of coffee is standing, and once heat from the cup has warmed the cognac, some sugar is added, and it's briefly ignited. The cognac is then poured into the coffee from the saucer.

Popularly regarded as the definitive example of the genre, Irish Coffee (see page 126) was created during the 1950s by barman Joe Shendan at Shannon Airport in Ireland. At that time, transatlantic flights had to stop and refuel at Shannon, and passengers were allowed to disembark for refreshments. To offer them more than just coffee, Shendan added a local touch: a measure of Irish whiskey. The black coffee was sweetened with brown sugar, and crowned with lightly whipped cream. No stirring is allowed, with the idea being to drink the hot coffee through the cool cream – and it really is a great idea.

irish coffee

Hot water for warming glass

25–50ml (1½–3½ tbsp) Irish whiskey

½ tbsp brown sugar, or to taste

Hot, strong black coffee, to top up

1 tbsp whipped cream

Pour hot water into a heatproof glass, then discard the water. Pour in the whiskey and sugar, then add coffee to within 3cm of the rim. Spoon in some cream so that it floats on the surface, and drink the coffee through the cream. No stirring! For a lighter option, use steamed milk instead of cream.

bourbon on the boil

45ml (3 tbsp) bourbon
1 tsp caster sugar
85ml (6 tbsp) boiling water
2 tsp lemon juice (optional)

Pour the bourbon into a heatproof
tumbler and mix in the sugar. Pour in
the boiling water and add the lemon juice,
if using. Stir before drinking.

coffee still

25ml (1½ tbsp) Mount Gay's Extra
    Old rum, or other aged rum
15ml (1 tbsp) Galliano liqueur
½ tbsp sugar syrup, or to taste
Hot black coffee, to top up

Pour the rum into a heatproof tumbler
or coffee cup, add the Galliano and stir in
the sugar syrup. Top up with black coffee.
Stir before drinking.

galliano hot shot

The intriguing flavour of Galliano is just as
effective combined with coffee as spirits.

20ml (1½ tbsp) Galliano liqueur
20ml (1½ tbsp) hot black coffee
Single cream, to top up

Pour the Galliano into a shot glass. Gently
pour in the coffee so that it 'floats' over
the top and does not combine, by pouring
it over the front (inward-curving side) of
a spoon. Then gently add cream in the
same manner to create a layered effect.

havana machiato

25ml (1½ tbsp) Havana Club three-year-old
    rum, or other premium gold rum
Hot espresso coffee, or strong black filter
    coffee, to top up
Dash of steamed milk
1 tsp caster sugar, or to taste

Pour the rum into a coffee cup and add the
coffee. Add some milk and sprinkle in
some sugar, then stir.

hot buttered rum

50ml (3½ tbsp) dark rum
25ml (1½ tbsp) lemon juice
25ml (1½ tbsp) apple juice
2 tbsp sugar syrup
Boiling water, to top up
Knob of butter
Garnish: ground cinnamon

Pour the rum into a tall heatproof glass,
then add the lemon and apple juices and
the sugar syrup. Stir and top up with
boiling water, then float the butter onto
the surface. Once the butter has melted,
sprinkle on some ground cinnamon.

hot mochalate

25–50ml (1½–3½ tbsp) coffee liqueur
Hot chocolate, to top up
1 tbsp whipped cream

Pour the coffee liqueur into a coffee
cup or heatproof glass, and top up
with hot chocolate. Spoon over the
whipped cream.

hot irish

Hot water, to warm the glass
½ slice lemon, studded with 4 cloves
25–50ml (1½–3½ tbsp) Irish whiskey
½ tbsp brown sugar, or to taste
Boiling water, to top up
Garnish: ground cinnamon

Pour hot water into a heatproof glass to
warm it. Discard the water. Add the lemon,
whiskey and sugar. Top up with boiling
water. Stir in the sugar with a cinnamon
stick and garnish with ground cinnamon.

left: irish coffee *top right:* hot irish

hangover cures

Is there such a thing as a hangover cure? So far, I've tried all sorts of things and the most successful healer is always time. With the worst hangovers, it's easier just to submit, accepting that any major activity, like getting out of bed, is going to be an ordeal. And if the entire day is a write-off, at least I can take comfort from the fact that tomorrow I'll be back to normal.

The inevitable question: 'Was it worth it?' is always a difficult one, particularly if total recall isn't possible. What's painfully obvious is that the severity of hangover symptoms – pulsating headache, nausea, dizzy spells, perspiration, tremors, and so on – operate on a sliding scale, reflecting the quantity of alcohol consumed. Moreover, the full toxic impact of ethyl alcohol, the intoxicant in alcoholic drinks, is only experienced around eight hours after the more immediate influence has worn off. Ironically, regular drinkers can cope better than the occasional binger, as their systems become more attuned to dealing with toxins.

Despite the fact that a hangover is an unavoidable chemical reaction, there are people who repeat with great authority that it's the quality of the alcohol that matters, and that, consequently, drinking the finest brands won't give you any problems.

Really? Forget it. However superior the quality, it doesn't alter the alcohol content, although the type of alcohol can make a difference. As vodka is distilled at a higher strength than other spirits, it does, in fact, contain a lower level of congeners, the impurities that cause hangovers. Nevertheless, this quality also depends on the amount consumed. Another refrain posing as knowledge is: 'Don't mix the grape and the grain' – a reminder not to drink grain-based spirits such as vodka, gin or whisky in conjunction with grape-based drinks such as brandy. Needless to say, being confined to one category or the other is hardly going to prevent a hangover if you go on a blinder.

The only way to prevent a hangover is, of course, not to drink excessively. Or at least not to drink just alcohol. Classic prevention tactics involve plenty of water, milk, or even some olive oil to line the stomach on the basis that this slows down the rate of absorption of alcohol into the bloodstream. But these safeguards also require forethought and discipline – whereas drinking sessions that go the distance tend to be spontaneous, rather than part of a considered masterplan. Drinking plenty of water is the best bet, solving the problem of dehydration, although it usually means frequent wake-up calls during the night. As the core of most hangovers, dehydration is caused by the liver using up vast amounts of water to break down alcohol, which acts as a diuretic. Moreover, many of us may already be in the dehydration zone even before hitting the bottle. The recommended daily intake of water is one-and-a-half to two litres daily, with even more required to compensate for coffee and alcohol. Drinking water continues to help the next morning, particularly in conjunction with vitamin C.

Traditional remedies such as the Prairie Oyster (see page 132) are not only endorsed by folklore but also by medical opinion. While recipes vary, a typical line-up of ingredients includes olive oil, tomato ketchup, Worcestershire Sauce, vinegar, Tabasco, egg yolk, salt and pepper. The egg yolk is key, being the ultimate in convenience food and easy to digest, providing vitamins A, B, D and E, as well as minerals like iron. Another remedy capitalizing on egg yolk is *caldo*, a Spanish chicken broth. At Christmas and New Year's Eve, many Spanish households have a pot of *caldo* ready on the stove. It is also served at *ferias*, around three or four o'clock in the morning, as a form of first aid to anyone who has over-indulged.

Sometimes any amount of liquid just isn't enough, and a great big helping of comfort food is the best medicine. A fried breakfast that pools the resources of eggs, bacon, sausages, black pudding and the rest, provides a typical British refuge. In Mexico this role is undertaken by *chilaquiles*: left-over tortillas are thinly sliced, laid in a casserole dish and covered with chicken, or other meat, and favourite accompaniments such as tomatoes, onions and chillies.

If rehydration, traditional remedies and a sustaining meal still fail you, then maybe it just has to be more alcohol. 'The hair of the dog that bit you' has long served as a mantra for hangover victims. It stems from an ancient Roman belief that if you were bitten by a dog, you should singe one of the dog's hairs and drink it in a glass of wine to guard against any possible ill-effects.

If a hangover is caused by cocktails, and the hair of the dog theory followed, then the 'hair' should also be a cocktail. And a cocktail called Corpse Reviver (see page 132) inspires hope even among the worst casualties. Originating in 1920s Paris, three versions have been in circulation, with the original recipe remaining as the standard: cognac, orange juice, champagne and a drop of pastis. Corpse Reviver No. 2 appears in *The Savoy Cocktail Book*, published in 1930, with legendary bartender Harry Craddock describing it as equal parts lemon juice, Kina Lillet, Cointreau and gin, with a dash of absinthe. He also added a cautionary note: 'Four of these taken in swift succession will unrevive the corpse again.'

One of the most renowned hangover cures, and my favourite, is the Bloody Mary, although it can be just as effective in causing hangovers. Its prototype may have been the Red Snapper, created by Ferdinand Petiot before the Second World War, either at the American Bar in the Ritz, or Harry's New York Bar, both in Paris. The Red Snapper combined gin with tomato juice, cayenne pepper, lemon juice, salt and pepper in such proportions that the spiciness of the cayenne balanced the sweetness of the tomatoes. Following the end of Prohibition in the US in 1933, there was a shortage of experienced bartenders, as many of the finest movers and shakers had gone to work in Europe. The owner of New York's St Regis Hotel hired Petiot to work at the hotel's Great King Cole Bar where his Red Snapper soon became popular. After the Second World War, when American palates began to embrace vodka in a major way, the recipe dropped gin in favour of vodka. It was also renamed Bloody Mary, and proclaimed as the ultimate hangover cure. The Bloody Mary may also have originated in the American Bar in the Paris Ritz around 1953. The bartender, Bertin, was asked by Ernest Hemingway for a tomato juice because his wife, Mary, would be monitoring his breath for signs of alcohol. Bertin suggested spiking the juice with a neutral style of vodka – no aroma, no giveaway. The deception worked, and on subsequent visits the drink gained its familiar cast of seasonings, as well as the name Bloody Mary.

A Bloody Mary (see page 133) is a perfect balance of vodka, tomato juice, Tabasco, Lea & Perrins Worcestershire Sauce and lemon juice, seasoned with salt or celery salt, and freshly ground black pepper. Tabasco and Lea & Perrins are essential seasonings, and both pre-date the Bloody Mary by a significant margin of time. But it was worth waiting as this cocktail presents them with one of their finest roles. Lea & Perrins Worcestershire Sauce was launched in 1837. The original recipe, which included vinegar, anchovies, tamarind, onion and garlic, was brought back from Calcutta to England by Lord Marcus Sandys. He then asked a local chemist shop, which was run by Mr Lea and Mr Perrins of Worcester, to make up the recipe for him. And from Worcester, Lea & Perrins set out to conquer the world. Tabasco, meanwhile, was created in 1868 by banker and bon vivant Edmund McIlhenny, who had a passion for condiments, spices and sauces. He grew Mexican peppers on the family estate of Avery Island near New Orleans, and his experiments with them produced the recipe for the renowned sauce.

A formula as enticing as the Bloody Mary inevitably led to experimentation, with popular extras like sherry, horseradish sauce and a celery stick garnish. The recipe can also be tailored using flavoured vodka, such as Absolut Peppar from Sweden featuring fresh jalapeño chilli pepper and paprika; Russian Pertsovka based on red and black pepper pods, and cubeb berries; or the Polish Pieprzowka flavoured with Turkish bell peppers and black peppercorns. The Bloody Mary has also developed its own 'bloody' genre. The Bloody Caesar substitutes clamato (tomato and clam juice) for tomato juice; the Bloody Bull adds consommé; a Bloody Maria uses tequila; while a Bullshot means vodka with consommé instead of tomato juice. So if one version doesn't provide the haven you need, perhaps another will.

corpse reviver

10ml (½ tbsp) cognac
30ml (2 tbsp) orange juice, chilled
40ml (2½ tbsp) champagne, chilled
5ml (1 tsp) pastis aniseed spirit

Pour the cognac into a champagne flute,
then pour in the orange juice. Gently add
the champagne and the pastis.

cubista

1–2 dashes Tabasco
50ml Havana Club three-year-old rum,
   or other premium aged rum
150ml tomato juice, chilled
To season: cayenne pepper, lemon or lime
   juice, Maggi sauce (optional), salt and
   freshly ground black pepper

Place a dash or two of Tabasco in a tall
glass, then pour in the rum and the tomato
juice and stir. Season to taste with cayenne
pepper, some lemon or lime juice, Maggi
sauce, if using, salt and black pepper.

gemada

*This Portuguese remedy combines the
nutritional benefits of egg yolk, the instant
energy of sugar and the sheer relief of stout.*

1 egg yolk
2 tsp caster sugar
Stout, to top up

Place the egg yolk in a tall glass, pour
in the sugar, and stir well to combine.
Top up with stout.

breakfast martini

Ice cubes for shaker
75ml (5 tbsp) gin
1 tsp Tiptree orange marmalade,
   or any other premium marmalade
Drop of Grand Marnier orange liqueur
Garnish: twist of lemon zest

Into a shaker half-full with ice cubes, pour
the gin and add the marmalade. Add the
Grand Marnier and shake, then strain into
a Martini glass. Garnish with the lemon zest.

miss branca

30ml (6 tsp) Fernet Branca bitters
10ml (2 tsp) white crème de menthe
   (mint liqueur)
10ml (2 tsp) cognac

Pour the Fernet Branca into a cocktail
glass, then add the crème de menthe
and cognac.

prairie oyster

Dollop of tomato ketchup
1 egg yolk
Dash of Worcestershire Sauce
Dash of Tabasco
Salt and black pepper

Pour ketchup into the bottom of a Martini
glass, or a saucer-style champagne glass.
Place an egg yolk on top of the ketchup,
then coat with the Worcestershire and
Tabasco sauces, and season to taste.
Consume using a small spoon.

seltzer

A few ice cubes
50ml (3½ tbsp) Wyborowa
   or Extra Zytnia vodka, or other
   premium grain vodka, chilled
25ml (1½ tbsp) lime juice
50ml (3½ tbsp) still mineral water, chilled
4 tsp sherbet effervescent powder

Place a few ice cubes in an Old Fashioned
glass or tumbler, then pour in the vodka,
lime juice and mineral water. Sprinkle over
the sherbet and stir in.

top left: *breakfast martini* **right:** *original bloody mary*

original bloody mary

2 ice cubes

40ml (2½ tbsp) vodka

4 drops Tabasco

8 drops Worcestershire Sauce

10ml (½ tbsp) lemon juice

Celery salt, to taste

1 grind of black pepper

70ml (5 tbsp) tomato juice, chilled

Garnish: slice of lemon or stick of celery

Place the ice cubes in a jug, pour
in the vodka and add the Tabasco,
Worcestershire Sauce and lemon juice.
Sprinkle on some celery salt and grind
over some black pepper, then pour in
the tomato juice and stir for a minute.
Pour into a tall glass and garnish with
a slice of lemon or stick of celery.

non-alcoholic drinks

The reply to 'Would you like a non-alcoholic drink?' could easily be 'What's the point?' The point, however, is to enjoy fantastic combinations of flavour that are an attraction in their own right – and not merely a consolation for the lack of alcohol. Indeed, alcoholic cocktails minus the alcohol provide numerous opportunities for rewarding drinks; my favourite conversion is the Bloody Mary to the Virgin Mary, more evocatively titled the Bloody Shame. Nevertheless, it does prove that the missing ingredient – in this case vodka – needn't diminish the appeal.

The enormous success of the Cosmopolitan (see page 26), made with vodka, cranberry juice and lime juice, and the Sea Breeze (see page 29) – vodka, cranberry juice and grapefruit juice – has, ironically, helped to promote cranberry juice as a party contender in its own right, with its wonderfully refreshing, rich but dry character. As one of the few indigenous fruits of North America, cranberries were prized by Native American Indians for their nutritional value, as well as their healing properties. Wounds were bathed in cranberry juice, and a cranberry poultice was used to draw poison from injuries caused by arrows. The Indians introduced cranberries, as well as corn, squash and sweet potatoes, to the Pilgrim Fathers, which helped

them to survive their first winter – hence the inclusion of cranberry sauce in the traditional American Thanksgiving Dinner. The Pilgrim Fathers also gave the fruit its modern name in the 1620s; as the cranberry's pink blossom resembles the head of a crane, they called them craneberries.

The range of traditional non-alcoholic cocktails, or mocktails as they are sometimes called, like the Pussyfoot (lemon, lime and orange juice, grenadine, egg yolk and soda water), has been extended in recent years by a whole new genre, combining radical chic with the ultimate in health consciousness: the dietetic cocktail. The rules for making these cocktails are rigid, and there's very little room for manoeuvre. Apart from a total ban on alcohol, dietetic philosophy also prohibits any form of sugar – and a 300g cocktail won't total more than 300 calories either. What a dietetic cocktail does contain is a maximum of five ingredients. These include fresh fruit juices and puréed vegetables such as fennel, spinach or celery, mineral water and flavourings like Lea & Perrins Worcestershire Sauce. This style of drink is already such an institution that the leading barmen in Europe have competed for the Annual Dietetic Cocktail Trophy, which is held at the Domaine du Royal Club Evian in France, since 1989. Having been a judge at this event in 1998, I can confirm that even such a disciplined regime produces drinks that will irradiate any happy hour.

An irresistible sense of nostalgia is helping elderflower cordial charm the British palate, just as it has done, on and off, for centuries. And if all the claims made for elder's medical prowess came true, the world would be a far healthier place. No more colds, hay fever or constipation, and insomnia would be nothing more than a bad dream. Every part of the elder has been used to prepare drinks – the flowers, berries, the leaves and bark. The price of such an asset? It's actually free – from a hedgerow near you – as long as you're there at the right time. Elderflowers usually arrive on the scene at Whitsun, with the creamy white flowers lasting until around the beginning of July. Infusing the flowers yields a cordial with a rich, lightly honeyed, moscatel aroma and flavour, together with a clean, lingering finish. Any elderflowers that remain unpicked have a great future ahead of them, as they develop into berries that turn from green to purple, and finally black. It's a simple colour-coding that indicates the berries are ripe for making into elderberry cordial.

Numerous other berries, fruits and nuts around the world invariably end up inside a bottle. On the Greek island of Hios, almonds are ground up, and a cloth is used to wring out the juice which is bottled, then served diluted with water. This is a traditional toast at engagement parties; ultra-white in colour, it's perfect for pre-nuptial celebrations. The refreshingly tart flavour of mauby, a speciality of Barbados, is prepared by boiling bark from the mauby tree (*Colubrina elliptica*), which is native to the West Indies. But there's no need to go bark picking. Someone else can do all that for you because bottles of mauby are widely available at local supermarkets.

In India, the choice of drinks offered to guests is dictated by the season, with cooling drinks in summer, and warming drinks in winter. Whatever the time of year, this also means non-alcoholic drinks throughout the day, as alcohol is reserved for the evening, with the custom being to serve guests very promptly – in fact, within a few minutes of arrival. The archetypal summer thirst-quencher and lunch party drink in southern India and Sri Lanka is the juice from green coconuts. Known as tender coconut, it is served as a long drink on the rocks, sometimes garnished with a chunk of coconut meat, which can be eaten afterwards, making the drink much sweeter. Also popular is tamarind with cold water, flavoured with sugar cane segments and curry leaf blossoms called neem.

In western India, refreshment is usually a matter of sar: fresh coconut milk infused with kokum, which is the rind of this sun-dried sour fruit. Milking a coconut entails grating the meat, briefly infusing in hot water, then wrapping it in muslin and wringing out the liquid. Known as the first extraction, this yields a rich, creamy milk which is reserved for cooking. The procedure is repeated to give a second extraction of thinner milk used to prepare the sar itself. Infusing with kokum turns the milk a delightful shade of pink. A pinch of cumin seeds and green chilli is then tempered in a little hot oil for about 30 seconds, before being poured into the sar. A favourite aperitif, sar is also served with curries.

In the north of India, summer weather is accompanied by a sherbet or Nimbu Pani (see page 139), literally, lime water, comprising lime juice, salt and sugar, diluted with water. It is customary to offer guests a lassi, usually at 11am. Lassi is also drunk with food. Each region in the north has its own particular way of preparing lassi; in Bombay, yoghurt is whisked or blended with a little water, which is then seasoned with a pinch of salt, black pepper and roasted cumin seeds, and garnished with coriander leaves. Sweet lassi also has a yoghurt and water base, flavoured with sugar and a pinch of salt. A speciality of Lucknow is thandai: lassi mixed with sugar and ground almonds, and garnished with almond flakes. Thandai means 'cooling', because that's exactly what it does, and is particularly popular during Holi, the Festival of Colour, during the spring equinox in March. Another feature of this festival is a symbolic colouring of the house, not to mention people, with coloured powder to signify the spring renewal. Children even add coloured powder to their water pistols.

A sherbet is essentially a concentrated infusion, and *panna* (mango) is one of the most popular styles served in Indian homes. Made by boiling mango pulp for 30 minutes to one hour, adding sugar, salt and possibly cardamom, the resulting liquid keeps in the fridge for up to a week. When guests arrive, all that needs to be done is add water, plenty of ice and a garnish of mint leaves. On India's west coast, sherbets make the most of kokum, which is also used to sour the region's seafood curries. Among professionals, particularly the renowned sherbet-wallahs of Jaipur, the range of flavourings is far more extensive, from vetiver and rosewood to ginger and saffron.

Fruit juices are a staple throughout India, with many stalls in every city. It's simply a case of picking individual fruit, or a combination of whatever's available, then stipulating the quantity of each. Fruits are peeled and juiced in an instant, seasoned with salt and pepper, as well as a dash of lime, if desired.

A typical winter brew in India is *massala chai* (spiced tea), with favourites such as ginger or cardamom pods added to the tea leaves, served with milk and sugar. Tea is a favourite with truck drivers, who pull up at roadside stalls and order it 'by the mile'. The theory is that different strengths of tea will keep the driver going for certain distances, and so stall holders have several variations constantly on the boil. If you hear a driver asking for a 50-mile tea, you know he's still a long way from home.

moroccan mint tea

(Makes 1 medium teapot)

Hot water for warming pot

1 tbsp China tea leaves

Boiling water, to top up teapot

Fresh mint, to taste, plus extra for garnish

3–4 white sugar cubes (optional)

Pour some hot water into a medium-sized teapot to warm it, then discard the water. Place the China tea in the pot and pour over a little boiling water. Add the mint leaves, and sugar if using, and top up with boiling water. Allow to infuse for a few minutes, then serve in small heatproof glasses. Garnish with a sprig of mint.

axis passion

A handful of crushed ice

50ml (3½ tbsp) orange juice

50ml (3½ tbsp) pineapple juice

50ml (3½ tbsp) double cream

15ml (1 tbsp) grenadine

½ banana, peeled

Garnish: slice of orange

Place the crushed ice in a blender, then pour in the juices, double cream and grenadine. Add half a banana and blend for 10 seconds. Serve in a Highball or tall glass, garnished with a slice of orange.

flamingo

5–6 ice cubes

70g clementines, peeled

60g apples

30g grapefruit, peeled

20g strawberries

20g white celery

To make this dietetic cocktail, put the ice in a blender and add the fruit and celery. Whizz for about 30 seconds then strain into a cocktail glass.

gingered apple

A few ice cubes

50ml (3½ tbsp) apple juice

Dash of lime juice

Ginger beer, to top up

Place the ice in a Highball or tall glass, then pour over the apple juice. Add the lime juice and top up with ginger beer.

leche merengueda

(Serves 3–4)

1 litre milk

3–4 tbsp caster sugar, or to taste

1 cinnamon stick

Finely pared zest of 1 lemon

Pour the milk into a saucepan and add the sugar, cinnamon and lemon zest. Stir and heat gently to boiling point, stirring from time to time. Turn off the heat.

Cover the pan and leave the milk to cool, allowing the flavours to infuse. Once cool, refrigerate for at least 4 hours. Serve very cold, in tall glasses.

long ginger

A few ice cubes

125ml strong ginger tea, sweetened
    to taste with honey and chilled

15ml (1 tbsp) lime juice

Place a few ice cubes in a Highball or tall glass and pour over the chilled tea. Drizzle in the lime juice and stir.

nimbu pani

A few ice cubes

Juice of 1 lime or lemon

Pinch of 'black' Indian salt, or table salt

Pinch of roasted and ground cumin seeds

Still mineral water, to top up

Place a few cubes in a Highball or tall glass and pour in the lime or lemon juice. Add the salt and ground cumin seeds, then top up with mineral water.

moonlight

Ice cubes for shaker, plus extra to serve

25ml (1½ tbsp) grapefruit juice

25ml (1½ tbsp) cranberry juice

25ml (1½ tbsp) orange juice

25ml (1½ tbsp) apple juice

15ml (1 tbsp) grenadine

Garnish: a few raspberries and cranberries

Into a shaker half-full with ice cubes, pour the grapefruit juice then add the cranberry, orange and apple juices and the grenadine. Shake well. Place a few ice cubes in a Highball or tall glass then strain over the juice mixture. Garnish with the raspberries and cranberries.

In an ideal world, where every party is perfect, all drinks would be served from exactly the right glasses

and prepared with a complete range of accessories. But that doesn't mean you can't compromise and

make a substitution here and there. That's why the recipes state alternative options wherever possible,

so that you know what to turn to if you don't have a Highball or an Old Fashioned glass to hand.

author's acknowledgments

The author would like to thank: Jenni Muir, Helen Ridge, Alison Barclay, Stuart Cooper, Clare Limpus and Maxine McCaghy at Conran Octopus, Jan Baldwin, Joanna Triay, Rena Salaman, Emi Kazuko, Namita Panjabi, Maria-Jose Sevilla, The Mexican Embassy, Agros, Swedish Trade Centre, Finnish Tourist Board, Russian Tourist Board, Bols, De Kupyer, Wray & Nephew, Brazilian Embassy, Hammond & Deacon, Chilean Pisco Association, Su-Lin Ong and Remy & Assoc, Jaspar Eyears and Cairbry Hill of Alchemist Management Services, Champagne Information Bureau, Hungarian Tourist Board, Finnish Bartenders Guild, Dutch Bartenders Guild, Harry's Bar, Venice, Underberg, CMA German Food Organization, Rupert Wilkinson at Malcolm Cowen .

For recipes, thanks to, in London: Jaspar Eyears and Cairbry Hill of Alchemist Management Services (whisky zen, balalaika, pina colada, brave bull, sake 1, sake martini, decibel, fj, prairie oyster, bull shot, seltzer, breakfast martini, michelado, planter's punch, killer zombie); Gilberto Preti, Duke's Hotel (diamond martini, red eye); Stefan Guichateau, Nobu Restaurant (mei-fuwa, nobu blackcurrant sake); Ben Reed, Met Bar (french 75, bellini, chocolate and orange martini, pineapple martini, fruits of the forest martini, sapphire martini); Orlando Hill, Brazilian Embassy (caipirinha, batida); Salvatore Calabrese, Lanesborough Hotel (black martini, christmas martini); Momo (moroccan tea); Marco Li Donni, 10 Room (flatliner); Maxwell's Group (roadhouse); Dick Bradsell (polish martini, hot buttered rum, mui rico); Ben Pundole (daiquiri, raspberry daiquiri); Guilio Morandin, The Dorchester Hotel (mirage, cosmopolitan, pink panther, dorchester coupe aux fraises, dorchester golden fizz, snow white);

Paulo Loureiro, Claridge's Bar (blue hawaiian, gemada, strawberry flapper); Jonathan Wallace and Giuseppe Ciarico, Brown's Hotel (cardinale, st george's fizz); Reece Clark, Fifth Floor Bar (sea breeze, harvey floorwalker, champagne cocktail, ocean drive, mudslide, dry martini, nutty martini, double vision), and Foundation Restaurant (rising sun, chateau cardillo) at Harvey Nichols; Laurent Vilaine, No 1 Aldwych Hotel (woo woo, mai tai, lynchburg lemonade, grasshopper, axis kiss, axis passion, moonlight); David Greenwood, Four Seasons Hotel (josephine, frankie, sterling silver, champanska, perfect martini); Danny Smith, Che (pomegranate and hibiscus margaritas); Namita Panjabi, Veeraswamy (nimbu pani, salted lassi); Havana Restaurant (la habana, cuba libre, mojito, havana machiato, cubista); Johnny Rosenthal (shandy no. 2); Atlantic Bar & Grill (loretto lemonade). Also, Joanna Triay (leche merengueda, sangria); Harvey Nichols, Leeds (Perfect Manhattan); Absolut (absolut angel), Agros (bison sour); Angostura (the charger, trinidad cocktail); Beefeater Gin (gin & sin); Berentzen (sunny samba, apfel cha cha); Bols (sweet city); Bulmer's (christmas glow); Chartreuse (france angleterre, champs elysées); Chilean Pisco Association (pisco sour, pisco fruit, chilean manhattan); Cointreau (margarita); Cooley Distillery (irish rickey); Campbell Distillers (ice berg, high flyer, perroquet, pastis riviera, tomate); Linie Aquavit (aquatini, the viking, mountain creek); Clément Rhum (rum rum punch); Finlandia Vodka (caipiroska, cranberry fields); Finnish Tourist Board (finnish summer bool); Galliano (harvey wallbanger, long slow comfortable screw up against the wall, galliano hot shot); Guinness (black & tan); Irish Whiskey Information Bureau (hot irish, irish coffee); Janneau Armagnac (armagnac daisy); Jagermeister (jager tonic); Lejay Lagoute (montana, flashing fizz);

Midori (margarita, harakiri); Mount Gay (coffee still); Oddbin's (peruvian pisco sour); Pimm's (pimm's rose and turbo); Plymouth Gin (bronx); Scotch Whisky Association (rob roy, whisky collins, loch almond, highland fling, long hot summer); Swedish Food Board (glogg); Toussaint (papa toussaint). In France: The Paris Ritz (miss brand, bloody mary, olympic, cp); Domaine du Royal Club Evian (flamingo). In Italy: Gianni Jianotta, Grand Hotel, Florence (green moon); Walter Bonzonella, Hotel Cipriani, Venice (angel's cup). In the US: Fifty Seven Fifty Seven Bar, New York Four Seasons (orange martini); Kentucky Distillers Association (old fashioned, bourbon on the boil, southern eggnog); Hakusan Sake (hakusan haiku); Maker's Mark (mint julep); Wild Turkey (bourbon sour). In Singapore: Raffles Hotel (singapore sling, million dollar cocktail). In Mexico, Presidente Inter-Continental, Guadalajara (sangrita).

publisher's acknowledgments

The publisher would like to thank: John Wallace, Paula Hardy, Marion Moisy, Olivia Norton, Keith Davidson, Kathie Gill and Nick Strangeway.

The publisher would also like to thank the following photographers and picture agencies for their kind permission to reproduce the photographs in this book:

2 Walter Chin; **6** Hulton Getty Picture Collection; **8** below D. Richards/The Telegraph Colour Library; **10** Victor de Palma/Black Star/Colorific; **12** above John Paul Urizar/Vogue Entertaining; **16** above Hulton Getty Picture Collection; **16** below David Loftus; **17** Chris Chen/Vogue Entertaining; **22** Mark Luscombe-Whyte; **24** Gilles de Chabaneix (stylist: M. Bayle) Marie Claire Maison; **25** Minh & Wass;

30 Miryam Bleeker/Taverne Agency; **38** Hulton Getty Picture Collection; **40** The Telegraph Colour Library; **41** Phillippe Diederich/Colorific; **46** Tony Stone Images; **48** Melanie Acevedo; **49** Tom Webster/Impact; **52** Hulton Getty Picture Collection; **62** Dennis Stock/Magnum; **66** H. Horenstein/Photonica; **69** Ernst Haas/Hulton Getty Picture Collection; **72** Peter Davidian/Photonica; **75** left E. Simanor/Axiom; **75** right Mike McQueen/Impact; **83** Margaret River/Belle Magazine; **86** Oliviero Olivieri/Condé Nast Traveller/Condé Nast Publications Ltd; **89** Antoine Bootz; **92** Marie Pierre Morel (Stylist: G. Reyre) Marie Claire Maison; **94** Tony Stone Images; **100** Vogue Entertaining; **103** Hamish Park; **108** Earl Carter/Vogue Entertaining; **114** Eric Morin; **116** Vogue Entertaining; **122** VNU Syndication; **125** Vogue Entertaining; **128** Hulton Getty Picture Collection; **131** Ronald Grant Archive; **136** Jeni Payne; **142** above left Hulton Getty Picture Collection; **143** right Inge Morath/Magnum.

Every effort has been made to trace the copyright holders for recipes and photographs. We apologize in advance for any unintentional ommission, and would be pleased to insert the appropriate acknowledgment in any subsequent editions.